The Affecting Presence: An Essay in Humanistic Anthropology

The Affecting Presence

AN ESSAY IN HUMANISTIC ANTHROPOLOGY

Robert Plant Armstrong

UNIVERSITY OF ILLINOIS PRESS

Urbana   Chicago   London

Frontispiece: Ifa Divination bowl, Yoruba. From the collection of Professor and Mrs. William R. Bascom

for my teacher and my friend, WILLIAM R. BASCOM

Contents

vii

Illustrations

Note: Illustrations are listed with figure title first, followed by the city or the artist, and then the tribe. When the tribal name is in parentheses, the term preceding it is the artist's name; in all other cases, the tribal name is preceded by the city. Where a dash appears, an element is missing.

Introduction

I have long been interested in the unconscious dimensions of man's behavior, and in none of them more than in
that highly generalized order of phenomena which one comes
to grips with when he asks the question, "What is it that is
Romantic in the arts of the Romantic period of European
civilization?" or "In what respects are 'classical' arts 'classical'?"
Most particularly, since various kinds of answers, most of which
are well known to thoughtful men, have been offered to these
two questions, I have been concerned to ask, "What is it in
African arts that is specifically African? Can I designate certain
undeniably 'African' features?" Naturally after some reflection
I saw that asking my question at the level of that which is
"African" made it practically impossible to answer. I therefore
posed it to myself in terms of the Guinea Coast cultural area,
that deep rich strip of African cultures lying between the Bight
of Biafra and Guinea, and finally in those terms that are, in the
last analysis, where one must begin—the arts of a single people.
For this purpose I have chosen those magnificent and ancient
creators of arts in West Africa, the Yoruba of Nigeria.

But my journey to the understanding of the arts of the Yoruba
entails more than just identifying them. In the first place, it
begins in a kind of feeling. This is not a very usual point of
departure for works in the social sciences these days—and yet
this is a work in social science; in anthropology, to be more pre-

cise. Like any other anthropologist, I am concerned to illuminate a basic and universal aspect of man's culture; to show something of its nature, its significance, its dynamics; and to demonstrate in the first place that the activity is patterned, which makes it cultural, and in the second place that that patterning is specific so that such patterns exhibit from culture to culture marked variations.

So I began with feeling, and then I proceeded to Nigeria—strangely enough by way of Java, and living a year in Java gave me that basis in feeling which eventually led to my first perception of the arts of a culture as, in a very specific sense, a unitive phenomenon. What I mean by this will become clear as I proceed. For the time being, let me say merely that I perceived after awhile what was Javanese about Javanese arts.

But as all know who have worked intensively with any problem, the problem itself is protean; it is richly ramifying and insists upon declaring itself, making itself known, defining itself in its richness, complexity, and subtlety. That of course is because a genuine problem is an organic, natural phenomenon. It enlarges reality for us, once it has posed itself and been described and answered. Forever thereafter it exists in its total statement as a portion of reality.

In the case of *the problem* which defines itself and is addressed in this book, I have naturally had to go beyond the point where I was led by feeling and by my Javanese experience. It has been necessary to examine those phenomena under investigation in ways which reveal their fundamental nature—What kinds of phenomena are they? How do they exist in the world, and what do they constitute in it? What is the structure of this resultant reality? By what method does one study it, and what are the implications of its study for the larger science of man? Finally, what is uniquely revealed about the work of art by such procedures? For unless something is disclosed which hitherto has been unknown—indeed even unsuspected—the problem has been only a form of conceptual cliché, its pursuit a dry exercise, and its results if not negligible at least worth little of one's time and expended energies.

Roughly the first half of this book is devoted to all but the last two of these questions, to whose resolution the latter half is dedicated. I have been criticized for this approach, and I greatly respect the intelligence and the motivation behind that criticism, for it was intended that if followed, it would yield a better book. I agree that it would have been preferable to "give the data first," but at the same time, I could not so proceed. It has seemed to me that even at the risk of losing readers, I cannot present the data *meaningfully* until I have considered carefully in the abstract (to which I have been led by much and earlier contemplation of the data themselves) some of the ontological questions relating to the work of art. In a word, I cannot provide the data until I have provided analytical concepts which I must subsequently use in presenting the data. If the reader wishes, since he will by no means find the data incomprehensible to him (only some of its implications), let him turn first to pages 101–86, then after that commence with the first pages.

The point of view developed herein, while not wholly unique, is both individual in its formulation and novel in its application. Since I am a publisher, I hope that my authors will derive some satisfaction, and perhaps even a little amusement, from the fact that I have been greatly influenced by their works. The broad enrichment of intellect which comes to one simply by virtue of the fact that he publishes diverse kinds of books is at least gratifying.

One should after all be intellectually and spiritually enriched by what he does to make a living. Notable in this respect is the fact that I have been privileged to publish in English many of the chief works in phenomenology. I have read in the field only as I have published in it; but though my study has not been programmatic, it has been revolutionary. If what I do in this book is touched by phenomenology, it is because my reading has persuaded me that in this philosophy lies the only option open to the anthropologist if he is to quit what seem to me to be the arid precincts of dull and profitless behaviorism and emerge into a study of man that is blessed with those meanings that do justice to the dignity, the subtlety and richness of man himself. Certainly it is true that no discipline can be taken fully seriously which purports to study man and does not stand finally face to face with these *qualities on their own terms*. Phenomenology enables one to do precisely this since it leads one to perceive phenomena not in simple terms of frequency, duration, direction, and other such "quantitative"—and more often than not accidental—categories, the real relevance of which is often difficult to apprehend, but instead to perceive them in terms which are inherent in the nature of the object of consciousness and of the process of consciousness itself.

The view I develop of the work of art as a thing in itself, with its own significance incarnated within its own existence and not external to itself—that view which rejects the notion of a work of art as a symbol, somehow involved with reference— is phenomenologically sound. This view seemed inevitable to me some time before I began reading phenomenological works, for much else that seemed true of the work of art would follow only if such a view were adopted. The phenomenologists have greatly sharpened this concept for me.

Some other ideas I also developed independently, only to discover them more crisply stated in the writings of the phenomenologists. A case in point is the idea of inter-medial equivalence which Maurice Merleau-Ponty developed in his essay "Eye and Mind":

Anyone who thinks about the matter finds it astonishing that very often a good painter can also make good drawings or good sculpture. Since neither the means of expression nor the creative gestures are comparable, this fact [of competence in several media] is proof that there is a system of equivalences, a Logos of lines, of lighting, of colors, of reliefs, of masses—a conceptless presentation of universal Being. The effort of modern painting has been directed not so much toward choosing between line and color, or even between the figuration of things and the creation of signs, as it has been toward multiplying the systems of equivalences, toward severing their adherence to the envelope of things.[1]

It is, however, not only to the phenomenologists, nor solely to those authors I have published, to whom I am indebted, nor to those who have reached conclusions similar to my own. The latter class is most notably exampled by the distinguished and careful work of Robert F. Thompson, who has through painstaking and sensitive fieldwork come up with conclusions concerning the Yoruba criteria for affecting excellence which in some instances are consistent with my own and in others identical.

[1] Maurice Merleau-Ponty, *The Primacy of Perception and Other Essays* (Evanston: Northwestern University Press, 1964), p. 182.

They can, therefore, logically fall within the argument of this book, a fact which I am compelled to regard as external validation of my concepts, methods, and results. Two specific cases in point are his observations concerning the Yoruba preferences for smoothness of surface[2] and for the avoidance of having things "sticking out." It may well be that I have misremembered on this last point, for I cannot cite a source for the observation. But if this observation has not been made, then it might as well be. As may be discerned subsequently, both it and the principles of smoothness of surface fall within what I shall isolate and identify as the discipline of intensive continuity.

It will be immediately obvious, I suspect, why I describe this book in the subtitle as being one in humanistic anthropology. This means that I am herein not only concerned with those areas of human activity with which humanistic studies have long dealt, but I am further concerned with them in terms of those very qualities and values which constitute their existence. In the long run it is this matter of approach which distinguishes the humanities from the sciences,[3] and not merely subject matter. Social scientists have, after all, directed their attentions to the arts for some decades now—though never to them *as arts,* for this cannot be done in the extrinsic terms which the social scientist is interested in using. And his extrinsic terms, on the other hand, are directly and very properly related to extrinsic problems, for his concern is not with art as it essentially is, but is rather with art as indicative of other dimensions of human behavior.

But this is not the place to become involved in the differences between the sciences and the humanities. Let it suffice to say that one friend who has said of my study that it is more "humanistic" than "anthropological" is, I fear, drawing a false dichotomy. The study of man and his works under the sign of human culture is an area of subject matter, not an approach to that subject matter. It can only be said of this study, if one wishes to use a

[2] Robert F. Thompson, "Esthetics in Traditional Africa," *Art News* 66 (1968).

[3] For an excellent discussion of this read Henry B. Veatch, *Two Logics: The Conflict between Classical and Neo-Analytic Philosophy* (Evanston: Northwestern University Press, 1969).

kind of oppositional rhetoric, that it is more humanistic than it is "social scientific."

In the long run, I think, it is profoundly anthropological—as I shall doubtless state several times again—to demonstrate the cultural dimensions of man's universe of feelings. To reveal order refuting chaos and the radical reduction of entropy which is culture patterning, to do this in an area where such has seldom been demonstrated, and in ways that are novel but duplicable—this I view not only as anthropology but as a signal recharge of energy for an otherwise tired and, to me, decreasingly compelling study.

Because I am sensitive to the criticism that commencing with the concepts and subsequently proceeding to the data may cost me some anthropological readers, I should like to provide a rapid overview of my argument. I adopt this course because I am persuaded that the keen pertinence which I believe adheres to those discussions in my book may be not lost, to be sure, but somewhat less compelling because of the necessarily careful method of procedure. A brief overview will surely indicate the critical centrality of their purpose.

Symbols are vehicles of meaning whose physical natures are arbitrary. The symbol's physical shape thus does not bear any necessary identity to its meaning. This is of course perfectly obvious, but it is too often the case that one does not use this conclusion as a starting point from which to seek to understand the nature of the work of art. And it is clear that one cannot reach an understanding of the work of art as part of human culture unless one knows what the work of art is. One's view, thus, has consequences.

It is the case on the one hand that works of art are physically identical to their "meaning," and on the other hand that works of sculpture, let us say, of a given culture bear to one another certain relationships of clear familiality. If these works were symbols, because the physical forms of symbols are arbitrary, neither of these facts would necessarily be the case. That they are both true is indicative of the fact that they are not symbols but rather are some other kind of phenomena. They are, I argue, actual presentations of the life of feeling. Further, because all the arts of a relatively homogeneous culture can be shown,

xviii

mutatis mutandis, to be physically identical in certain significant ways, the case is further strengthened and the way is
prepared for one to develop the systemic view of the arts of
man. The universe of man's feeling is thus opened to our contemplation and inquiry, and this, added to what we have observed of his overt, interpersonal behavior and the products
of his universe of thought, yields a fuller and thus more reliable
view of man.

But if the work of art is not a symbol, what then is it? Borrow-
ing from certain of the arts, I call its ultimate principle *metaphor,*
a concept which has been used widely and with increasing
diversity of meaning. Philip Wheelwright has given a most
useful analysis to the term, and he distinguishes two senses
of the word, one of which he calls epiphor after Aristotle's
usage in the *Poetics,* and by which he means that which expresses "a similarity between something relatively well known
or concretely known (the semantic vehicle) and something
which, although of greater worth or importance, is less known
or more obscurely known (the semantic tenor) . . .[4] it does not
follow that the similarity need be obvious nor the comparison
explicit."[5] In the other sense:

the essential possibility of diaphor lies in the broad ontological fact
that new qualities and new meanings can emerge, simply come into
being, out of some hitherto ungrouped combination of elements.
If one can imagine a state of the universe, perhaps a trillion years
ago, before hydrogen atoms and oxygen atoms had ever come together,
it may be presumed that up to that time water did not exist. Somewhere
in the later vastitude of time, then, water first came into being—when
just those two necessary elements came together at last under the right
conditions of temperature and pressure. Analogous novelties occur in
the sphere of meanings as well. As in nature new qualities may be
engendered by the coming together of elements in new ways, so too
in poetry new suggestions of meaning can be engendered by the
juxtaposition of previously unjoined words and images. Such diaphoric
synthesis is indispensable as a factor in poetry.[6]

It is indeed the indispensable factor in the other forms of art as
well.

Metaphor, as I view it, is at one and the same time both the

[4] Philip Wheelwright, *Metaphor and Reality* (Bloomington: Indiana University Press, 1962), p. 73.
[5] Ibid., p. 74.
[6] Ibid., pp. 85–86.

mode of being of the affecting presence and its only category of "truth." Metaphor is thus the essence of the work's being, its ontological quintessence, and the basic nature of metaphor lies in the fact that a medium which is after all one sort of physical thing—say *sound,* or *color*—is transmuted into something wholly different, from discrete insensate physicality to sensate life. The former estate, insensate physicality, is characterized at the one extreme by that condition in which random instances of the medium meaninglessly occur (in terms of the affecting presence) and at the other by structures, which are meaningful in the same affecting frame of reference. This is to say that there is critical difference between a grunt and a formula; between an occurrence of red, and the red of the flag of the U.S.S.R. In these instances the physical data are insensate—they do not have the characteristics of life: they are not dynamic; they do not "metabolize"; they do not extend the reality of a subject, directing consciousness toward one and inviting one's own consciousness in return. It is this which characterizes the estate in which items of physical media become bits in a whole work which is forever—and forever in the same way—sensate.

As I have pointed out above, however, it is further the case that metaphor is more than the mode of being of the work; it is its category of truth as well. Perhaps I am being needlessly complex here since it is obvious that if something exists in a certain mode then all things pertaining to it must also be in or closely related to that mode. In any case, not only is it true that in the affecting presence the mutely physical is made eloquent, but it is further true that data from all media can be so transformed—and *even further* that there are, in all probability, systems of equivalence[7] among the various media. It may well be that such equivalences are less truths than tautologies. In any event, the simple fact of the matter is that metaphor, that estate in which something which is of one sort becomes of another sort, is the ontological ultimate of the affecting presence and constitutes its sole universe. "Truth" thus lies in the fullness of existence of the work, as well as among the various equivalences. As is characteristic of all other areas of man's life, the use of metaphor is both structured and patterned.

[7] Merleau-Ponty, *Primacy of Perception,* p. 182.

Metaphor, finally, is the *being* of the work of art; through metaphor it exists. When the anthropologist studies art, he studies not the detritus of behavior or the strange products of reason gone awry, but the actual, incarnated being of the non-verbal, affective life of man. Thus it is that the time-honored method of the anthropologist, to *inquire* of his informants about the work of art in culture, is in the vast majority of cases both irrelevant and misleading; since inquiry proceeds from erroneous views, it cannot produce relevant information and it can only obscure our fuller views of man.

It is against this conceptual background that I proceed to examine in some detail the arts of the Yoruba and, by way of contrast, those of the Javanese—though these in considerably less detail.

There remains only the pleasant honor of acknowledging those who have been helpful to me in this enterprise.

I am indebted to relatively few people for the work represented in this book, and thus I do not expose many to the blame for whatever flaws exist herein. There are a few friends, however, I should like to acknowledge: Professors Alan P. Merriam and Roy Sieber of Indiana University, Professor John Povey of the University of California at Los Angeles, and Professor Alvin Wolfe of the University of Wisconsin at Milwaukee have been interested in my developing views and have on several occasions given me the challenge to develop my views further by inviting me to address their seminars in the African humanities. Professors James Fernandez, Daniel Crowley, Arnold Rubin, Dr. Justine Cordwell, and I have for years discussed the problems of studying African art; and I am much indebted to them, especially to Professors Fernandez and Crowley, who read this essay while it was yet in typescript, offering valuable suggestions. My occasional discussions of African art with Professor Frank Willett have also been inevitably rewarding. I wish especially to thank Miss Anita Glaze, Mr. Michael Quam and Mrs. Millicent Quam, Mr. Charles Adams, Mr. Emmanuel Odita, and Mr. Stephen Wild, who, one evening after a seminar at Indiana University, went with me to The Poplars in Bloomington where they questioned me and, quite without their knowing, helped determine me to write this book. Mrs. Jeanne Beemer, my secretary, did more than type several drafts of this work. Her careful attention to detail has made for a better book. Miss Jane Phillips has edited the book with uncommon skill, and has earned my professional respect as well as my personal gratitude. There are obligations of a more personal nature I must also acknowledge, notably to Warren E. Frey and to my mother, Dr. Josie M. Trinkle.

Finally, I record with great pleasure the interest which the Program of African Studies of Northwestern University, in the persons of Professors Gwendolen M. Carter and Ibrahim Abu-Lughod, has shown in the humanities and especially in this work for the completion of which the Program awarded me a grant.

Robert Plant Armstrong
Evanston, Illinois
1970

The Affecting Presence: An Essay in Humanistic Anthropology

Affecting Things and Events

Were it not for the fact that the meaning of the word has become so muddled by now, I would say that the topic of this book is art—art and culture. But "art" is a term so charged with varying values, so diffuse in its designations that it can have little utility. I want to be quite sure that it is understood what kind of phenomena I shall be discussing, and "art" gives no promise of advancing such understanding. For this reason I am electing to avoid the traps of the past—as they are hidden in this word at least—preferring instead to come up with a designation I feel to be more useful, if only for the reason that it is new and thus free of the tyrannies of a confused semantic life. But I would seek a word or term that had more than this to recommend it—one that serves to describe what a certain class of objects and events *is* rather than one that tries to indicate the presence or absence of that state of special grace which when present makes one object "art" and another, sometimes surprisingly like it, "not art."

I shall seek that designation from among those words that belong to the area of feeling, or affect, since—to go directly to the heart of the matter—I believe that is the domain of the things we shall be concerned with. For this reason, and for the present, therefore, I shall speak of *affecting things and events,* which are those cultural objects and happenings resulting from human actions directed toward producing *them* rather than anything

3

else, which is to say that they are not accidental. These objects and happenings in any given culture are accepted by those native to that culture as being purposefully concerned with potency, emotions, values, and states of being or experience— all, in a clear sense, *powers*. Further, irrespective of such considerations, under certain circumstances and in some cultures such things and events may be admired for the excellence of their own properties; thus, this admiration is in itself of an affecting nature. In other words, such things and events are characterized by some people in some cultures as having "beauty." These affecting things and events may be *depictions* of subjects, objects, and states of affairs, or they may be *abstractions* from or *variations* upon such subjects, objects, or conditions. In any case, they are regarded by those co-cultural with them, thus *appropriately* regarded, as being in and of the real world, however constituted, including the mythical.

The "powers" with which these affecting things and events are concerned tend not to be clearly separable one from the other in any specific thing or event. Indeed, these categories may, and often do, simultaneously characterize an affecting thing or event. A sculpture, for example, may be asserted to have potency and thus to accomplish good, yet at the same time forcefully constitute the abstraction derived from the contemplation of the form or significance of a hero. The concepts of potency, bravery, force, and hero clearly produce affect, and it is to this affect that the thing or event is dedicated, and thereafter is the work, affecting us when we enter into transaction with it. By *work*, which is the body through which the act of presentation occurs, I mean the thing or event as a depiction of, an abstraction from, or a variation upon an object, an event, or a theme in the internal or external world achieved by means of the affecting media, those components of volume, movement, and experience which eventuate in the affecting work. These media are subsequently described herein. (See pp. 15–19.)

Each such work, which is in enduring media, is a perpetual act because it is self-contained and wholly committed. Those which are in evanescent media become perpetual when recorded. The totality of such acts constitutes a separate universe —not of discourse, but of feeling. This is the domain of *presen-*

tation [1] and the ultimate objective of the creation of things and events in the affecting universe. Presentation, not representation, is the goal of the artist; even though representation is sometimes achieved, this is another and quite different function of the work—not necessarily an *affecting* function, irrespective of the fact that emotional attachment may exist between the model for and the perceptor of the work.

Because such works are perpetual and perpetuating acts— the act ever in the process of being enacted—I find it accurate to speak of the *affecting* things and events. By the use of this participial form, I intend to convey the idea that the perpetual and perpetuating act is also perpetually and perpetuatingly in affect. It is thus to be seen as a very special kind of action that is of concern here; and as action, it is particularly recommended to the serious attention of all students of human action and behavior. Affecting things and events are not negligible doodads in culture but constitute a distinct and significant category of human existence. If understanding of this category is not achieved, it follows that there is no full understanding of human behavior, and the social sciences are solely of society— not of man—and thus incomplete.

Inherent to this approach is the creator's intention to produce a work conveying affect. To introduce intention as a criterion may offend those who have thought that the "intentional fallacy" was once and for all removed from the world of criticism. But especially in the area of exotic art, the intention to produce affect is probably essential to the identification, in some instances at least, of the relevant things and events. Thus the bull-roarer (fig. 1) of the Australian aborigine might be thought simply to be a noise-maker and his churinga (fig. 2) but a decorated paddle if one did not carefully ascertain by ethnographic inquiry that the intention in making the former is to strike terror into the hearts of the uninitiated, in connection with certain rituals, and the intention in making the latter is to create an object of considerable spiritual significance. In any case, one can justifiably maintain to the person who accepts "art" but who berates the relevance of intention that

[1] Susanne K. Langer, *Philosophy in a New Key: A Study in the Symbolism of Reason, Rite, and Art,* 3rd ed. (Cambridge, Mass.: Harvard University Press, 1957).

5

the latter is easier to determine, as the case of the churinga demonstrates—even if interiorized, as it often is—than "art" is to identify as a category of human products. This is particularly the case from the point of view of the anthropologist.

The above is aimed at the defense of intention as a criterion in the process of identifying those things and events which will constitute a class of works roughly analogous to "art." In addition, I have mentioned, however briefly, something of the *how* of going about the determination of the presence of the affecting. But these remarks have neither raised nor responded to the very important consideration of *why* intention is important in identifying affecting things and events. The answer to this is not only simple, but it is also basic to our enterprise. There are many kinds of affecting works, but only some of these are intentionally created to be such. It is in these latter ones alone that we are interested. In the first place, there are some affecting things and events that are not created at all, but these are obviously outside the area of our interest if we are to isolate a class somewhat like but yet differently constituted from "art." A tree in Java or in Nigeria may be thought to house spirits and thus to be affecting; or a rock in Samoa may be said to contain power. Animals may be considered as being sacred, as may certain fruits and vegetables. A storm may fill one with terror if it is regarded as an expression of the wrath of a god. The criterion of intention thus helps us eliminate from our consideration natural things and events which have come to be affecting.

A very different problem is posed by the man-made thing or event which, while perhaps not having been created primarily for the purpose of being affecting, is nonetheless intentionally concerned with power, as an inevitable condition of its being what it is. An example is the host in the Mass, or the act of elevating it. The host was made to be transformed into the body of God, and its elevation is connected with this rite; thus, both object and act are intentionally concerned with power. But it cannot be said of either host or act that there is present any intention to create a work, in the sense in which that term is here used; it does not, as we shall see later, proceed by metaphor *to be*. The host is presentation uncloyed, if it is presentation at all—which of course is the question. But it is one which is easily resolved, for I have defined presentation as being

6

1. Bull-roarer, Australia.

brought about through a work. And since neither host nor elevation is a work, the power believed to be resident in the host cannot constitute an act or condition of presentation. It cannot be a
work because its form is not necessarily related to, and is not a
condition of, its being.

The bull-roarer, or rather its sound—for that is the important
affecting function of the instrument—represents yet another
case. The terrifying sound of the bull-roarer is made with the
clear intention of affecting. It is the transmutation of a material;
it is not the sound of the paddle roaring through the air which
one hears, but the veritable voice of a totally different essence
which has come to be. In this case, as in the transubstantiation
of the host, a reconstitution of the material is brought about;
but the intention is not only to make the essential quality of
the event affecting, it is also to have an actual work, an event,
composed of affecting media. This is the kind of phenomenon
we wish to study. The voice of the bull-roarer is an affecting
work, as clearly as the B-Minor Mass of Bach; and yet it is
most unlikely that anyone other than those informed by the
views represented here will perceive it as such. The other
things and events—the churinga, and the host and its elevation
on the one hand (which are intentionally affecting but are not
works and presentations), and the rocks and trees on the other
hand (which are affecting but not only are not presentations or
works, but also lack intentionality)—will be of interest to the
person who wishes to study the affecting world. For our purposes, however, such phenomena must be omitted.

It is thus clear that both *affecting things and events* and
intentionally affecting things and events as categories admit
the inclusion of more things and events than the *affecting works*
category, the one with which we are here concerned. It is also
clear that these three categories among them adequately classify
phenomena of the affecting universe and that they will thus
serve the analytical purposes of the anthropologist, who must
place together into common classes all things and events which
share common characteristics.

It is not too difficult to determine the presence of the intention to be affecting. Interrogation, of course, is one way. Perhaps
it is even the best way. But there is another method as well.
Frequently such objects and events as are intended to be in-
vested with feelings are accorded special treatment—they are

8

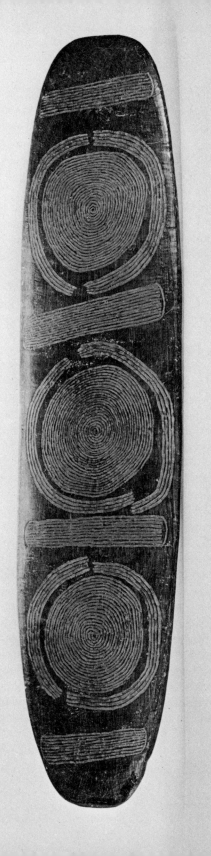

2. Churinga, Australia.

placed in galleries or in shrines; they surround important persons; they are used in rituals; or they are hidden away from public gaze and ordinary use. The factor of special treatment indeed becomes a key one in the interrogation of informants. Any informant who is at home in his culture will know whether in any respect a given thing or event is special and whether it deserves the kind of treatment which indicates an investment of feeling—whether it is held in awe, whether it receives sacrifice, protection, ritualized respect, or indeed disrespect, as in the case of the stone Nomoli figures of Sierra Leone (fig. 12) which are beaten if the crops that are in their care turn out to be less good than they are expected to be.

In contrast to this inductive approach, it would prove unrewarding to proceed in an investigation based upon the notion of art, and the beauty which presumably is its foremost characteristic, for "art" is difficult to communicate as a concept, to say nothing of "beauty," and would not make a useful basis from which to organize one's inquiry. To attempt to study the affecting things and events of another people by using the concepts of "art" and "the beautiful" would constitute a surpassing example of ethnocentrism, the exportation to an alien context of our own values, our own structures, our own grid. And yet there are numerous instances in which anthropologists, those professionally most sensitive to the subtle insistencies of ethnocentrism, have themselves ethnocentrically used "art" to categorize certain phenomena. Whether as a result of their lack of clarity about what "art" is in their own culture, or out of some residual determination to be sensitive to the variability of data, they have sometimes tended to emerge with a congeries rather than a class of things and events—when they have included events at all. Their congeries have included non-affecting items from the material culture as readily as intentionally affecting ones, axes as readily as works of sculpture. As for "beauty," I have heard more than one anthropologist assert something to the effect that one could not convince him that the Yoruba, for example, have no notion of beauty; they must have—how else could they create objects as "beautiful" as certain figure carvings he has seen.

Quite as serious a problem is that which leads the anthropologist utterly to abandon himself to the social science fallacy —that argument which holds that all is behavior and behavior is all (or as the corollary runs: if there is anything else, we cannot really know it). This approach treats the affecting thing or event simply as thing or event—it causes the researcher to measure, to count, to sort, and to develop lists of motifs. Such study discloses the physical item to him, and something of its social dimensions, but reveals nothing of notable significance, nothing of the *affecting* existence of the things or events he studies. To such a worker, a sculpture may be an assemblage of traits, a symbol of social solidarity, an instrument for controlling the gods, evidence of trait diffusion, or an economic fact. It is all of these, to be sure. But there is missed here the identification of the one basic, critical, and inalienable fact, that the sculpture is an affecting thing. It is as though a person were to be defined (as he often is) solely in terms of his roles and physical characteristics without ever having it said of him that he is a man, a "me," a sentient and feeling human particularity. To have missed saying this of a person is to have missed saying anything at all that is really definitive, that is, in the last analysis, basically relevant.

The terms provided here must take the place of "art" and "beauty" in the analytical vocabulary of the individual who would identify and study a class of phenomena of which all the components, in any given culture, would share common, critical, definitive characteristics; and of the student who would define, in any given culture, a class of like-featured things and events which would bear the mark of the individuality of that culture and embody many of its powers.

We have established a category, or a class of things and events, based upon affect—feeling—and have maintained that these are works and that such works are intentionally affecting and are amenable to identification. It is also maintained here that the intentional creation of affecting things and events is a cultural universal. Even in those parts of the world where materials for such works are most rare, the creation of affecting things occurs. The Eskimos engrave ivory, and the pygmies of the Kalahari Desert decorate ostrich eggs—the vessels in which life-sustaining water is carried and which must therefore be greatly accompanied by feeling—and they also sing and dance.

But although the realm of affect is universal, there is great diversity among its works. Affecting things and events range from depiction to abstraction, from the passionate to the removed, from the extravagant to the austere, from the complex to the simple—not only from culture to culture, but also even within one culture. Today there is probably a greater degree of synchronic diversity in the affecting works of the United States, for example, than has ever before characterized the works of man. And there is an extraordinary diversity of the means of executing affecting works and a disposition toward experimentation to match and exploit that diversity.

But there is also diachronic diversity within one culture. Such movement can be seen in the history of the affecting works of European civilization, for example in those great shifts from the styles of the Middle Ages to those of the Renaissance, through Neo-Classicism, the Baroque, and Romanticism. Diachronic diversity does not characterize the works of European civilization alone, of course; one sees it as well in the history of Nigerian, Egyptian, Indian, and Chinese civilizations.

Perhaps it is my own closeness to the European tradition which makes the diachronic diversity of European works appear to be characterized by more dramatic shifts than the histories of works in these other civilizations. In any case, it has been well and often enough demonstrated that political, intellectual, and economic intercourse among European national groups facilitated the diffusion of innovations, and that there was a high degree of receptivity to foreign ideas, goods, and works. The fullest possible exploitation of one's environment and of one's self appears to have grown into a consuming passion with Western man, and the achievement of such maximal exploitation demanded universal heterodoxy, both synchronic and diachronic. It is thus that one accounts for the great diversity of affecting works. By way of contrast, one can look to the last millennium of the affecting works of the Yoruba of Western Nigeria. Though this history is far from exhaustively documented, it is sufficient to permit one to perceive its synchronic characteristics as well as the contours of its diachronic evolution. (See discussion on pp. 102, 122.)

The incidence of diversity of affecting works, both culturally and cross-culturally, is varied and rich. The complexity of synchronic diversity in contemporary America argues either heterogeneity of audience or rich development of the affecting self—the sensibilities—or both. Historical diversity bespeaks the value shifts, the affecting evolution of a people, from rich but austere order (the European Middle Ages) to a liberated humanism, for example. The inhibition of diversity, on the other hand, suggests either a spiritual constancy—a constancy of affect —or else a remarkable facility for maintaining stylistic continuity despite historical changes that must have brought about shifts in a people's circumstances. Of the two possible explanations, only the former seems acceptable.

It is also true of the works of the affecting universe that one cannot cross-culturally or cross-epochally predict the affecting content of works with any high degree of probable accuracy, though he may perceive features of which he may assert that they are doubtless of affecting significance. It is the case that one cannot identify the content not only because similar feelings may give rise to different styles, but also because similar styles may convey very different feelings and values.

Let us examine two comparable situations in which affective behavior (as distinct from affecting things and events) is clearly involved. In Jogjakarta, on the island of Java, bicycles seem as densely packed on the streets as do automobiles on a major Chicago expressway. If there is an accident on one of these streets, the two cyclists will smile, exhibiting all the graciousness they can muster, given the shock of the situation. On the other hand, should there occur on the Chicago expressway an accident involving two cars, the facial expressions of the two drivers would hardly express graciousness or bear smiles. Situations which are comparable, then, produce differing facial expressions, but we must question whether these "styles" also express different emotions. Indeed, we need not assume that the interior states of affect are totally different in the two instances. In both cases the parties must have experienced disruption of plans, as well as expense, trauma, and a certain amount of both anguish and pain. Therefore it is even true not only that the exterior situations are analogous but that the interior ones are as well. That such differences of expression should mark two situations bearing so many points of affective and physical similarity seems impressive evidence in support of my assertion.

We encounter the opposite situation as well. One may observe very close or even identical forms and yet not justifiably conclude that they convey the same affect. Let us take laughter, for example, which is a subtle and complex action in terms of its conveyed affect. In his own culture, a sensitive and intelligent

13

man doubtless has fair mastery of the subtleties and complexities of laughter, but such mastery does not necessarily equip
him for understanding the laughter of someone from an alien
culture. Thus we are not prepared for the Javanese laughter as
an alternative to interpersonal rudeness, nor will they readily
understand our laughter of derision. The meanings of laughter
are contextually determined, to be sure, and given this fact, I cannot fancy the American laughing at, rather than cursing, an of-
fending fellow motorist; nor can I easily imagine the Javanese
permitting himself the expression of derision as a solution to an
interpersonal problem.

The pyramids of Egypt and Mexico provide another example
in connection with affecting works. The forms are basically identical, but their functions are wholly different—the one was designed as a tomb and the other, a temple. In Egypt, the interior
of the tombs was exploited; in Mexico, the surface was exploited.
Drumming is predominantly used ritually in West Africa, but it
is rarely used ritually in contemporary American society. The
case is the same with dance, for despite the fact that dance has
of late been taken occasionally to the altar, one can hardly maintain that such dance is a prevalent or essential religious act.

As for instances of affecting works showing great diversity and
yet being clearly responsive to the "same" or closely analogous
feelings, one can point to the wide range of the varied forms and
works which embody the feelings of those who have developed
cults devoted to the ideas of "nativistic revival." This is merely
one example from the rich diversity which, throughout the world,
characterizes the works affiliated with the basic institutions of
society toward which one must assume that, despite cultural
variability, all men feel somewhat the same. There is the possibility that some might reject as unwarranted such an inference.
One can, after all, know of feelings only through the affecting
works we are discussing; only through them can we know
whether there is identity of feeling, for a given institution, among
the peoples of different cultures. And unless one is co-cultural
with a work, in all probability he can never truly be said to know
the feeling of the work.

Diversity is both inevitable and infinite in affecting works. In
this respect, affecting things and events differ from affective behavior. This must obviously be the case, for while the range of
physical possibilities for the expression of affective (and affecting)

14

behavior is limited, the possibilities residing in line, volume, tone, sound, movement, and color are infinite. Thus the face may smile or frown, the eyes may weep or gleam or be dull, the arms may droop in despair or lash out in anger—but these possibilities do not even begin to match the wide spectrum of potential exploitation in the affecting media. (See Table 1.) Even the body trained for movement in dance immeasurably enriches the lexicon of expressiveness, in contrast to that untrained body which is, in relative terms, mute. Because of this broad base for diversity, it would be most remarkable if in many instances affecting works from different cultures should turn out to be significantly similar. I am not, of course, talking about two peoples near to each other, such as the Dogon and the Bambara of Mali, whose works are, by all save the most judicious, sometimes easily—and understandably—mistaken one for the other. Correspondences in such instances where diffusion would inevitably bring about similarities can be ruled out.

Although it is a consideration of content rather than of form, if I may be permitted this spurious dichotomy, of special sig-

Table 1. Distribution of Affecting Media among Forms

	Sculpture	Dance	Graphic	Music	Architecture	Drama	Verbal Narrative	Costume	Poetry
Situation	X	X	X	X		X	X		X
Surface	X	X	X		X			X	
Color	X		X		X			X	
Volume	X	X			X				
Tone				X					*
Movement	X	X				X		X	
Word						X	X		X
Relationality	X	X	X	X	X	X	X	X	X
Experience	X	X	X	X	X	X	X	X	X

* I have omitted *tone* while recognizing that it exists in tonal language as an element—but of meaning, not of poetry.

15

nificance to this question of particularity and universality is the consideration of certain basic affecting units which often find their ways into affecting things and events irrespective of cultures, which sometimes exist in reverie and dream, or which frequently find explicit statement in religion. I am thinking of the remarkable distribution of the "light" and "dark" image clusters, where masculinity, day, life, rationality, the sun are attributed to the "light" side and femininity, night, death, emotionality, the moon, to the dark. It would seem that if we ascertained the particular charges of affect which accompany these clusters from one culture to the next, we would be singularly advantaged to carry out those studies suggested by these considerations.

But apart from such a human substratum as is suggested by this basic and pervasive symbolism, it is nonetheless the case that the possibilities of formal variability are so great that one overwhelmingly finds diversity rather than identity from one area of the world to the next. Because this is the case, and because both the student of art and the anthropologist perceive a recognizable familiality to the affecting works of a people, we must assume that there exists in every culture a "lexicon" of conventionalized conditions defined by the culture to be adequate to the task of being affecting, and a "grammar" governing their relationships. This system, which we do not call "language" despite the fact that we have used two linguistic terms, organizes the affective life in special, meaningful, and patterned ways and is itself a condition of affective being.

Whatever affecting powers the carved wooden figures of the Yoruba of Nigeria assert, for example, they assert them in a system composed of a limited degree of structural variability. In contrast with the nineteenth-century Parisians, and in respect to these affecting works, the Yoruba exhibit a narrow affective band. The Yoruba carve figures for use in ceremonies involving the gods or the ancestors—for worship, for divination, for prestige. The works are executed in a range of positions that show limited variation, and the parts—head to neck to trunk to limbs—exhibit clearly stated relationships of mass that are subject to rigorous and limited grammar. The narrow inventory of types of pieces is doubtless because the Yoruba artists seem to be carving for a few specific functions; that the types of figures show so little diversity is owing both to the fact that the style is demanding and that the carver appears to be carving generalized representations—Ifa

16

figures, and so forth (figs. 3, 4, 5). Their grammatical economy, however, is more difficult to characterize and to account for. It is to this characterization, or to a small part of it at least, that a later portion of this present work will be devoted. (See pp. 101–36.)

Intentionally affecting things and events exist in surface, color, volume, tone, relationality, word, and movement. To these I shall add *situation,* to accommodate works of narrative and dramatic dimensions, and *experience.* All these I shall refer to as *media,* and they are found in all intentionally affecting works as the means by which affecting is accomplished. These media are not significant, however, in accidentally or referred affecting works such as, for example, a sacred rock or the host in the Mass. Indeed they do not in any intentional sense characterize such symbols at all, but rather only those which may be called, according to our definition here, *works.* Further, the traditional divisions of "art," which we here call *forms,* are composed of these media.

I have regarded each of these media quite literally, so that there is no room for other than the strictest of interpretations. Thus, although there is, for example, the concept of "color" in music, and although it is of affecting import, this "color" is a property of tone and not a primary medium in itself. It is a phenomenon which derives its name figuratively, owing to its synaesthetic resemblance to color deriving from the use of pigment. "Movement" presents a similar case, for it is often said to characterize the graphic arts and architecture. But I have chosen to interpret the term solely as actual movement in time or space. "Volume" presents a somewhat different case, for I have indicated it as characterizing the graphic arts, in which I include all two-dimensional affecting works; obviously there are no volumes as such in a painting, for instance, but there are representations of volumes. This is the one liberty I have permitted, and it seems justifiable enough.

It must further be observed that the media I have indicated for each form need not all characterize every given product in that form. Significant volumes may or may not be used in costuming—they are not in *Les Sylphides,* but they are in the masks used by the Egungun dancers of Nigeria. Sculpture, the graphic arts, and architecture may or may not be characterized by color; sculpture exploits movement if it is a mobile, but otherwise not, and so forth.

17

All the forms, however, are characterized by relationality and experience. *Relationality* is intended to designate those relationships that come to exist among parts, either in time or in space. Rhythm is thus a phenomenon of relationality, as also are harmony, balance, symmetry and asymmetry, and dynamics. Relationality is that factor which makes a totality of the other elements, causing them to exist as a recognizable whole. It does not exist by itself as such but is rather a characteristic of other media—though it is subject, via the media, to conscious exploitation. Accordingly, relationality exists at a different level from the other media. But it is a medium nonetheless, for it is freely variable of the media, which is to say that if in two instances the exploited media remain constant except for relationality, which is in both cases different, two different affecting works result.

Experience, like relationality, characterizes every affecting work, but it is nonetheless variable with respect to the degree to which it is present in a given work. Further, it is a cultural variable—in a more subtle way than is any other medium. Experience is a complex of elements relating to values, and it alone is the cause of that flash of relevance, that quality of illumination which makes of the whole work a valuable and significant documentation of human being, suffusing the work with the processes of its own life. Obviously, like relationality, it is not itself a separate medium but is rather a condition of the work's existence, a state of affairs built upon the mastery of pertinence with which the other constituent media are controlled and expressed. This pertinence is a function of genius. It is related to what, for want of a more appropriate word reflecting its role in the affecting universe, we may call the actualization of the affecting *idea.*

Each of the media enjoys certain properties which are subject to variability and which are, therefore, the ultimate building blocks of the affecting work. It is these which provide the opportunity for more extensive, more complex, more subtle exercise of relationality and utilization of experience. Surface has extent, texture, finish; color has hue, value, chroma; volume has length, breadth, depth, density; tone has pitch, amplitude, timbre; movement has tempo, frequency, direction; word has sound, connotation, affect; situation has action, motivation, and sense and psychological detail; and relationality has dy-

19

3. Woman with twins, Ilesha, Yoruba. (front and back)

4. *Ibeji, Ila Orangun, Yoruba.*

namics and complexity. Further, the properties of the media are subject to concentration or dispersion—and this may be interpreted as maximization or minimization of spread in spectrum, tones, structure—and to continuity or discontinuity, terms which are intended to convey the notion of maximization or minimization of the possibility of straight-through spatial (line, color, movement, volume) or temporal (tone, situation, movement) development. All affecting things and events, then, are composed of constellated properties of media which, by the exercise of relationality, achieve experience.

Mention will be made of three of the "art" forms. First we will consider poetry, for although it shares with narrative and drama the medium of "word," poetry is concerned with the word as such, as an instrument in the creation of new experience as opposed to the depiction or reporting of situations that characterize both non-poetic drama and narrative. The interest in poetry is not in the *meaning* of the word, which is quite clearly beyond the word as such, but rather in certain properties of the word itself which are to be found on its affective periphery —such as ambiguities, "color," history—and which are woven into a fabric of partly conscious, partly unconscious feeling. Naturally there is a "poetic" dimension to narrative and to drama as well, to that extent to which these works exploit the affecting properties of the word itself, quite apart from its denotative functions.

There are two "arts" whose inclusion may strike one as curious—costume and dream. Costume, perhaps, will find acceptance relatively quickly, if not quite happily. Dream is likely to be another matter. But there is an affecting work of the unconscious, which is *dream*. Dream is, by its very nature, private self-drama, inner literature, not externalizable—limited in address to the interiority of one man at a time—never to be shared by another. Because it is inner, immediate, and cannot be universalized by virtue of being made equally and ever available to all, it is well to call it not an affecting presence, but an *affecting present*. But otherwise dream shares with the other forms constitution by rhythm, movement, and experience and sometimes by the feeling of line, color, and volume as well. If the other affecting works may be said to constitute the theater of consciousness, dream is the theater of unconsciousness.

Affecting things and events, in final sum, are perpetual affect-

21

5. *Ibeji, Ila Orangun, Yoruba.*

ing acts, existing via a limited number of media which are intentionally made to be what they are—always and primarily concerned with feeling. They proceed from depiction, abstraction, or variation to presentation intentionally and affectingly to convey subjects, objects, or states of being. Affecting things and events in a given culture systemically relate one to the other, such that it is a matter of definition that works from different cultures which resemble one another are not in all probability to be regarded as comparable unless the two cultures have related *systems* of affect.

Affecting works are not simply decorative, not odds and ends to be lumped together under material culture, nor amusing accidents or irrelevancies. Rather, they are self-contained actions which, once committed, are self-perpetuating, so that even exhumed after centuries of burial, they yet assert themselves in our presence. These acts are most relevant, most critical, most profound, most radical in their significance to an understanding of the whole of man. This ontology of the affecting work demands of the anthropologist that he perceive it for what it is and that he make every determined attempt to study it in relevant terms for what it is, which is to say as an affecting presentation, in addition to studying it for what it is not.

The Affecting Presence

The host in the Mass is affecting, but it differs from a sculpture or a musical composition in at least one significant way: the host is a symbol because it is intended neither that the host should in itself constitute a work in the outer and inner world, by virtue of the affecting media, nor that it should, by means of its form, have presentationality. It is clearly intended that the host should stand for something or, as the name suggests, *host* something. Thus the host is a symbol—an affecting symbol, intentionally created to be such and nothing either more or less or different.

The affecting thing or event with which I am concerned is, however, a very different kind of phenomenon. I have described it as a perpetual and perpetuating action, complete within itself. As such it is an actor, continuously in act, even though it acts only within a predetermined area and in a predetermined way. It is a part of being, continuously affecting when it is in the presence of a perceptor, for its affecting role is with respect to people whereas its nature as a committed action is perpetuated irrespective of perceptors.

But although the affecting work exhibits characteristics of actor and affectant, it is at best but a limited actor in that it cannot act beyond the limits of its restricted creation. It differs thus from a person, for although the affecting work is in many respects like a person, it is not a person, to be sure, for reasons

24

we see clearly but which we shall explore further. In recognition of the affecting work's special characteristics, I prefer to refer to the affecting work as a presence—an affecting presence—intending by the name to suggest something of its autonomy, its "personality," its existent and self-sufficient nature as an act and to recognize its relevance and its power to affect. This category of affecting materials excludes both natural objects and events as well as man-made affecting symbols.

The affecting presence acts as subject, asserting its own being, inviting the perceptor's recognition and, in culturally permitted ways, structuring that subsequent relationship which someone has called "transaction" in recognition of the fact that while the presence informs the man, the man, in his unique way, to some extent and in some fashion informs the presence. But although the presence is subject, it is a limited subject. Its limitations are described by its restrictedness, by the extent, indeed, to which it is at the same time an object. It obviously cannot perceive the perceptor; it can only be perceived, owned, created, and disposed of. It is not uncommon, however, to find that its sense of being is so acknowledged that the affecting presence is accorded special treatment—sometimes it receives the attentions and services accorded a person: it may, as is true of some of the sculptured figures and masks of West Africa, be bathed, clothed, fed, and, when its usefulness has ended, buried. Indeed, in certain kinds of magical situations, it can be "sickened," "deprived," "wounded," or "killed."

In the recognition of this quality of personality which characterizes the affecting presence lies the refutation of those who would deny the work's selfhood and maintain that it is not a presence as herein described but a symbol, carrying some meaning or feeling from the mind of the artist to the mind of the perceptor, with offhand rejection accorded the view that the work does not symbolize but *is* its own affecting.

The symbolistic fallacy is especially beguiling in those cases in which the affecting presence is a representation of some model external to itself. But representation, lying within the genius of all the media, is in this sole respect a burden that must be borne—or rather that representation may give rise to confusions is a situation to be abided. The affecting presence is perpetrated by an artist after an affecting "idea"; it is the artist who brings about the work, but it is the work that presents.

25

Once created, the work embodies the idea and, insofar as it is representation, its model is irrelevant to its existence—the work has also embodied the model. The artist is no longer important. Thus, the work stands in the relationship of immediacy, not of mediation, and does not fulfill the role of the symbol. Indeed, in the long run its frame of reference, as described by the affecting media, is—as affecting presence—solely itself. That there was a model in a different universe is irrelevant to the affecting presence in that special and self-contained world of affect. (The validity, indeed even perhaps the sense of much of what I am saying here, will be seen more clearly in the discussion of that network of metaphors which discipline and quicken the media and which tie the complex elements together into a vital whole.)

The affecting work, then, is an affecting presence, a self-contained, perpetuating actor on the one hand and a human-perceptor related affectant on the other. But there are other complexities characteristic of the affecting presence which must also be noted. In terms of its recognition by a perceptor, any affecting presence is universal, cultural, and particular. Inasmuch as the affective realm is universal, affecting presences may be expected to be recognized outside their producing cultures— not in terms of the specific nature of their affecting existence, perhaps, but identified as an affecting presence. To a certain extent, the attempt to perceive such works from an exotic culture *in their own terms* is probably of doubtful merit, problematic to accomplish, and perhaps characteristic chiefly of a highly educated and sophisticated culture characterized by intensive and frequent international, inter-cultural contacts. Nonetheless, at the very least, there might be identification of the forms of one culture among the peoples of a great many more cultures, irrespective of such "sophistication."

It is this aspect of universality which has led to many foolish statements by those who, knowledgeable of the arts but not of the important cultural and individual variables of man, have been beguiled into judgments and interpretations based upon the universal aspect. Such judgments have understandably alienated many anthropologists from much of the writing in the field of "primitive art" and have driven them to their own cautious statements, based upon close observation and abhorring the imaginative, as both an area of study and a technique in-

26

volving the leap into pertinence and revelation. As a result, anthropologists have tended to over-correct and have not written about the affecting presence as such at all. It is one of the purposes of this essay to place the study of such phenomena where it belongs, in the purview of the anthropological humanist, thus pleasing the art historian or critic who senses the universal, yet at the same time satisfying the anthropologist who wants cultural context and variables accounted for in the formulation.

The recognition of the affecting presence, I have mentioned, is universal. This is true in two respects—formal and emotional. In the first instance, recognition occurs because all peoples who create affecting works do so by virtue of either depiction of, variation upon, or abstraction from the perceivable world and its experiences, and therefore they recognize such depictions, variations, or abstractions as indicating the likely existence of a work characterized by a present affecting purpose. Similarly, one can often know when affect is present in a work by observing whether it is greeted by its perceptors with feeling, even though the exact content or the precise boundaries of the feeling may not be obvious.

Each affecting presence is inescapably individual; equally, by definition, all such presences are cultural, since together, in respect of their own kind, they constitute a cultural order of phenomena. In the instance of a given culture, however, *individualism* may be a cultural value, in which event both intra-form diversity and the radical differentiation of pieces are more highly prized than is the assertion of familial characteristics.[1] Late twentieth-century England, for example, asserts the desirability of the radical differentiation of pieces and of intra-form diversity more markedly than did Renaissance Italy, which, despite the marked differentiation of pieces by virtue of a style demanding individuation of subjects, nonetheless did not exhibit as wide a range of intra-form experimentation. In other words, the Italian Renaissance did not produce a situation in which there were simultaneously practiced styles as far apart as are primitivism, realism, surrealism, and abstract expressionism.

---

[1] By the phrase "intra-form diversity" I intend to suggest, with respect to music for example, the co-existence of different styles as well as of classified traditions and types of musical presences within these styles.

27

Although culture is a collectivity, it is also much more. It is not passive as a statistic is passive but viable as a master system from which one cannot escape and within which one finds his meaning, deriving his conscious knowledge as well as his unconscious attitudes and perceiving the world through its grids. The affecting presence is the tutor of our feelings, and that part of existence it teaches is capable of infinite instruction. Further, feeling is with us early—and it is articulate earlier than the intellect. It is, in fact, a primitive level of existence; and what relationship it has to thought, to the structure and content of behavior that is not affective, one cannot easily say. One can with safety assert that it is not irrelevant. I would be tempted to suspect that the way in which one organizes his feelings and the motifs he stresses are not at all unrelated to the rest of his life. This holds true for culture as well, for culture is man writ large, simultaneously both superman and supraman.

The feelings crave extension and definition of being as ardently as the mind, and thus one learns new affecting idioms—through experimentation, acculturation, and the rise of new philosophical attitudes, such as that of individualism in the Western world. In West Africa, prior to the last decade or so, the affecting works of any given type were characterized by little differentiation in any given tribal group. Representations appear to have been generalized and were, by and large, myth-related. Perhaps because myth is itself general, the sculptures had to be general also. In any case, the two generalizations of myth and affecting work were functionally related, and their reciprocity doubtless magnified the content and the force of the work. But today shows us that the more experimentation, individualism, and acculturation intervene, the more the individual is alienated from this coherent, affecting dialectic—from myth to form—and under certain circumstances a radical starvation of affect can occur and disorganization and affecting anemia can result. Of course, there can even be a free-floating surge of affect which, only vaguely known, seeks to create new and socialized works in order that it might, defined, emerge into being. Such, for example, were the works of the cargo cults which occurred notably at various places in the Pacific after World War II.

It would seem that one could take the existence of a body

of generalized social or mythic representations, exhibiting little diversity, to be indicative of a culture which in general is characterized by homogeneity with respect to its affective life, whereas the existence of radically individuated works could be indicative of diversity of the articulation and the content of feeling.

Affecting presences are culturized, by which I mean that necessary to the relationship between presence and person is the guided production within the person in culturally approved ways of affective responses, which are similar from one person to the next irrespective of happenings in one's own history that might, and indeed do, give added affective resonance to the experience. Since this is the case, works clearly do not lose their presentation, when they are deprived of their native audience, but do lose something of their originally intended presentation, and thus their native import. In such a case, an alien perceptor perceives with referred affect, accepting the affecting presence in those terms he reserves for what he presumes to be like works in his own culture. In such an instance, there might be something of that affecting which was originally intended, which is yet inherent in the transaction; but if this is so, it is the result of purely fortuitous convergences. Under such circumstances of being erroneously perceived, or reinterpreted, the affecting presence does not cease to be what it was created; it is simply confined to the slavery of misapprehension, of inapposite interchange.

Ontologically, the affecting presence is a perpetuating, affecting act—a near-being, with its unique "personality" continuously asserting its own existence, though it is known only in transaction. It is independent of any source of "meaning" or energy external to itself; being a self-sufficient entity, it is its own "meaning" and provides its own energy.

It is unfortunate perhaps that I have had to use Susanne Langer's term, for what I mean by the *"presentational* affecting presence" is different from what she means by the "presentational symbol," which is the term she decided upon to designate the "work of art." For Mrs. Langer, though the work of art is "non-discursive" and although no artistic medium may be thought of as a "language," the work is nonetheless a *symbol,* an instrument important in "conceptualizing the flux of sensa-

6. *District officer, Thomas Ona, Yoruba.*

tions,"[2] and an act of "reference."[3] The affecting presence, however, is not a conceptualization, nor does it in any intrinsic respect refer to anything at all—in no respect that is inherent to its nature, at least, although it may do so secondarily, or "extrinsically." On the contrary, it is actualization rather than conceptualization, and this not of the flux of sensations but of form via the flux of sensations, a form whose only significant apperception is in terms of feeling, for in feeling lies the only possible intrinsic meaning of the work.[4] Because "presentational" so fits the act of confrontation that characterizes the relationship of the affecting presence to its perceptor, the revelation which the former makes to the latter, I choose to use it here; and in my own mind, I reserve for Mrs. Langer's conception her alternative term, "non-discursive form," for insofar as it references, it seems not so much presentational as representational. It is this difference which removes the non-symbolic affecting presence even further from the question of language, which proceeds by conceptualization and reference, than the non-discursive symbol is removed from it.

The affecting presence is a thing-in-itself—a *presence* as I have called it here—and not a symbol because the creator does not build into his work cues to some real or imagined affective estate external to the work itself, but rather strives to achieve in that work the embodiment of those physical conditions which generate or are causative or constitutive of that emotion, feeling, or value with which he is concerned. What I am describing is a phenomenon much like that which T. S. Eliot referred to in poetry as the "objective correlative of an emotion." The meaning of the affecting presence—or more properly its "feeling"—is thus not external to itself. Naturally, it enacts its being only in interchange between itself and a perceptor, appropriately when that perceptor is co-cultural to it, probably wrongly when the opposite case is true.

One cannot say that the affecting presence is a symbol re-

---

[2] Susanne K. Langer, *Philosophy in a New Key: A Study in the Symbolism of Reason, Rite, and Art*, 3rd ed. (Cambridge, Mass.: Harvard University Press, 1957), p. 88.

[3] Ibid.

[4] It is also unfortunate that I must use "meaning," which refers to the world of reason and its devices, the symbols. However, I use the word on the principle of analogy, just as I did when I wrote of an "affecting idea."

ferring, as it were, to itself, for this is not what a symbol does, and thus one can no more say that an affecting presence is a symbol of itself than I can say of any person that he is a symbol of himself. The affecting object, on the other hand—the host in the Mass—does refer to something external to itself; therefore, it is a symbol. The sole relationship of an affecting presence is with its perceptor, and since when he encounters a work for the first time it is on the basis of absolute novelty, it can hardly be said that the affecting presence symbolizes that which comes into realization subsequent to the work's creation, for a symbol cannot symbolize what is consequent to it. Nor, finally, is a work a conceptualization; it is a concretization, and as such it is what it is. In transaction, it is the inseparable and inalienable outer half of an emotion in that affecting encounter involving people and affecting presences. An affecting presence is thus a presentational presence, and it is existentially "all there."

One may say, "all well and good as far as concerns the modern abstract expressionist, for example, but what about tribal art which is rooted in the most economical kind of functionalism? Can one maintain that the carving of an ancestor figure in West Africa is anything more than an act of reference? Can one say anything more of the twin figure than that it is a reminder of a human being, or that it has some sort of ritualistic function? Is it not the case, in other words, that the distinction between extrinsic and intrinsic does not hold for the Yoruba, let us say, and that all Yoruba art has extrinsic meaning only? Certainly field workers have not been able to demonstrate the existence of that intrinsicness which would suggest anything at all about the affecting presence in Yorubaland." I would reply to such an argument that it may be true that the field worker has not been able to demonstrate the existence of evidence sufficient to justify the existence of this quality of the intrinsic which is essential to the concept of the affecting presence—but it is just possible he has not known how to read the evidence which is about him in abundance! If one can demonstrate that formal discipline itself is of overwhelming importance and if one cannot find extrinsic reasons that satisfy him as explanations of striking formal interest, then one has evidence which must not be explained away by accepting such unsatisfactory answers as "we do it this way because our ancestors did," or "we do it because it looks better this way," or "there's no reason at all why we do it this way." Either this, or one must infer that there is a reason more profound than either the informant or the anthropologist has previously expected. This becomes a compelling conclusion when one perceives, as we shall subsequently, that what are in one sense identical formal themes are repeated not only time after time in one given form (sculpture) but also in all other forms (music, dance, narrative) as well. Under such circumstances, one will have demonstrated the existence of factors which are of overwhelming importance and which are not clearly relatable to extrinsic factors.

33

The Social and Physical Study
of the Affecting Presence

The affecting presence is complex and elusive to study, for it is simultaneously of three natures—physical, social, and affecting—all of which comprise numerous subtleties and, therefore, problems. The physical dimension, as we have seen, is composed of nine media and nine forms, in addition to the complexities of the properties of each medium. The social dimension is greatly complex, including considerations of the work's function, and the maker's and perceptor's interactional characteristics and powers as well as their placement in society. Finally, there is the affecting dimension whose complexities one must unravel.

Of these three dimensions, the social is wholly extrinsic to the affecting presence as such; the physical is germane, to be sure, but as yet only as gross, non-discriminated, and non-significant data. (*Significance* derives only from the meaningful perception and construction of gross physical data according to inherent principles governing such construction.) Of the three dimensions, only the affecting one is undeniably intrinsic. For the fullest possible view of the affecting presence, presumably, it is essential to seek a tripartite understanding considering each of these areas of existence. It is especially important to insist upon this, for there is a tendency among those scholars who have studied such phenomena to assume that when they have studied one aspect of the work's existence,

34

they have done all there is to do. Some humanists occasionally seem to believe that they have taken all relevant account of an affecting presence when they have studied it in its own terms, irrespective of cultural variables; some social scientists tend to assume that they have explained the affecting presence when they have described it as either a social or a physical event. This partialism is most beguiling in the case of the anthropologist who, tracing every dimension of social, religious, economic, and craft life that he can identify, often seems to suggest that he has given a complete account of the affecting presence, without stopping to realize the inadequacy of a notion of culture that does not deal with interiority, and without, at the same time, realizing that the affecting presence is most uniquely an address from and to man's interiority.

On the other hand, one's view may presumably be more nearly of the unique and thus in a sense of the most definitive properties of the affecting presence, ignoring however its behavioral and physical dimensions. In such a case, however, it follows that those affecting properties must be viewed in terms of some criteria other than those which are systemically *of* the culture, as when an inexperienced but sensitive European admires an African sculpture. Another view, further, neglects to take into account that the particular behavioral paths which are possible to trace all come to rest in a unique presence to which all the visible, behavioral data are not exactly irrelevant, but surely not in the final analysis definitive.

The social scientific study of the affecting presence is rationalistic and quantitative; it is "functionalistic" and essentially extrinsic to the work itself. The humanistic study is qualitative, evaluative, concerned with the interior dynamics of the work; but while it so confines its attentions to the work and to values and feelings, it is not exclusively or necessarily totally intrinsic. By *quantitative* I mean a concern with measurement and with the structural analysis of context; *extrinsic* refers to the direction in which this interest in quantification is taken, in this instance from the work outward to the context. By *qualitative* I intend to denote a concern with the thing itself, in its own terms, and whether the thing is good or bad, effective or pointless; and the *intrinsic* is the field of qualitative concern. *Functional* pertains to the fit of the work in its context, while *relational* refers to the inner-relatedness of the parts of the work. The view of the

35

affecting presence here developed entails intrinsic study, for the work is regarded as self-contained, self-sufficient, a presence in and of itself.

Our first attention, however, will be devoted to a brief mention of that extrinsic, contextualistic field of study, and concerning it I shall note but two studies—first that magisterial work of Alan P. Merriam, which provides the most rigorous program available for the extrinsic, social analysis of an affecting form.[1] This is not intended to be primarily a study of the affecting presence of any given people, but is rather a highly generalized work showing all the factors which must be taken into account if one is to give satisfactory address to the extrinsic factors of a musical work. It is not true that he gives no consideration to intrinsic factors, for he acknowledges their importance; but as this aspect of the field of study enjoys little significant development, there is not much for him to say. Robin Horton's *Kalabari Sculpture*[2] is a detailed study of the sculpture of the Kalabari of Nigeria and is, in a sense, a documentation in detail of many of the general points which Merriam raises. These two works are paradigms of the extrinsic—sometimes not quite accurately called "cultural"—study of the affecting presence. Yet neither of them in any important way gives recognition to the ontological status of the affecting presence which needs to be taken into account, for one must have a theory about the nature of the affecting work if he is to say something meaningful about it and about the inner reality of culture. Further, neither Merriam nor Horton exhibits marked concern with the analysis of the physical existence of the affecting presence, an inseparable aspect of the consideration of the work. Their attentions on the contrary are devoted solely to its social existence. Thus they place themselves within the anthropological tradition as it relates to the treatment of "art," a predictable and understandable bias in favor of social inquiry—predictable since the creation and continuation of the affecting presence are possible only in culture, and it is thus hardly surprising that the history of the study of such works has reflected a concern for them as social happenings. Looked at in another way, it is equally

[1] Alan P. Merriam, *The Anthropology of Music* (Evanston: Northwestern University Press, 1964).

[2] Robin Horton, *Kalabari Sculpture* (Apapa, Nigeria: Department of Antiquities, 1965).

36

not at all surprising that the most trenchant studies of affecting objects and events, outside those ancient centers of Europe, Asia, and North Africa that have long been involved in the patterns of world conquest, should have been made by anthropologists. It is they who, having moved outside these ancient centers of ferment, have perhaps most sharply discerned the significance of cultural variables in identifying, understanding, and evaluating an affecting work.

There is a range of problems to be studied under the heading of the social[3] dimension, and I shall briefly discuss those I see as pertaining most clearly to the social study of the affecting presence. Basically, this includes inquiry into techniques of execution, rules of ownership, questions of attitude, ways of understanding and judging, as well as all aspects of personal interactions that touch upon the achievement or continued existence of the affecting work as a social fact. The identification of the values, judgments, feelings, beliefs relevant to the work, as well as of meanings ascribed to it, is thus basic to a social study. All the foregoing problems may be generalized into studies of technique, function, and epistemology.

Technique

There is little to be said here in detail about the study of technique. There are numerous good studies of pottery, weaving, basket-making, and the production of music. I have seen films of carvers at work, and these document in a most effective way the manufacture of a work of wooden sculpture. One can also read excellent accounts of the lost-wax method of casting metal pieces. It is possible to document adequately the technique of the dance through film, for the "material," after all, is the human body in paced motion. The techniques of making narrative or poetry are more difficult to describe, since the actions of manufacture do not in any way involve the use of any significant external process.

Doubtless to be considered here also are studies into the at-

---

[3] I am avoiding calling such studies "cultural," for they can be considered so only by using the term with a license that tradition has permitted. But for the purposes of this study I shall use "cultural" only for those studies which are more holistic, taking into account the comprehensiveness of culture, including the affecting presence *qua* affecting presence.

titudes that accompany manufacturing. These have been adequately done as well and have addressed themselves to such questions as: What is the guiding pattern? What are the criteria of technical satisfaction? How does one learn the techniques, and from whom? What are the ritual obligations that must be discharged before the work can be undertaken or completed? Studies of technique, it is clear, are not concerned with affect.

Function

It is doubtful whether the anthropologist has discovered any functions of works of which the art historian, the critic, and the psychologist have been unaware. But he has been of paramount service to the field of study in demonstrating that these functions are fulfilled by objects and events in some instances strange—indeed even outrageous—to the sensibilities of those having had less broad experiences.

Throughout the whole range of culture, one finds only a limited number of social and individual functions served by the affecting presence. These include first the assertion of values, either individual or cultural. It is true, by definition, that individual values do not exist outside culture, and it is equally true that even the most conventionalized statements of group or social values will inevitably bear the mark of an individual hand.

Works primarily concerned with stating individual as opposed to group values (that is, self-to-self) are less widespread than those asserting general values. Generally these self-to-self works have been characteristic of those peoples with an abundance of leisure time, although it is not true that all societies with leisure time available produce such works. Works which assert social values, however, are as we have said more widespread, and they include the Statue of Liberty, the average plaster saint in the nearest church, and the ancestor figures in a West African shrine. These examples are intended merely to be suggestive of the kinds of works included in this function. Obviously many instances will arise in which it is possible only with the greatest difficulty to ascertain whether a work asserts social or individual values. In some cases, indeed, it may be impossible to tell, but this suggests the sharpening of the criteria rather than the abandonment of the concept.

A similar situation exists in music, dance, and literature (including drama and ritual) as well. Music for religious services, songs which are publicly valued and are assumed to assert social solidarity, religious or national dances, epics, liturgies, myths— these all have a greatly socialized function (in that their base of involvement is more generalized), and they contrast with Beethoven sonatas, the ballet *Interplay,* and Sheridan's *The Rivals,* just as Shango figures contrast with Ife bronze portrait heads, and plaster saints with Modigliani's portrait of the Lipschitzes.

There are functions in addition to the assertion of social or individual values: didacticism, delight, release of tensions, the maintenance of cultural vitality, the prevention of affective starvation, and what Ruth Benedict called "compensatory daydreaming." There are economic functions as well—such as costs and consumers; and there are religious and political functions— the use of the affecting presence in rites and ceremonies. It is clear that "function" analysis of the art of a people would yield a list of functions that would probably reach throughout the culture, bringing affect to bear—stimulating, awing, providing value significance—at many of the points of crucial cultural articulation. The affecting presence may indeed, in this truncated cultural sense, be regarded as that instrument which permits the objectification and manipulation of values and which is reinterpreted (the paintings representing Byzantine saints decorating an atheist's study) when the value conditions that produced them change, as is the case with simple utilitarian objects that are no longer useful, or cast out, as has happened numerously in West Africa in the face of the advance of Islam and Christianity.

Epistemology

The study of the values, feelings, beliefs, meanings, and judgments *relevant to* affecting works is by and large underdeveloped. One must here distinguish two classes of such considerations. Insofar as such factors are the direct burden of the affecting presence, they are most properly to be viewed as of concern to a discussion of the affective dimension of the affecting presence. Insofar as they are *about* rather than *of* the work, however, they properly come under a consideration of the social dimension. Examples of such secondary relevance are as follows: attitudes

40

toward the work, once it has been manufactured; judgments about its quality and effectiveness; theories, if any, about the nature and function of such works; the role of the work in ritual and belief. Many of these questions have been considered in a symposium held in Lake Tahoe in 1965 (Social Science Research Council conference on *The Traditional Artist in African Society*, under the leadership of Warren L. d'Azevedo), and when published the papers will constitute a basic source of information on the subject.

A study of these aspects of the affecting presence will yield ethnographic[4] placement of it as an object of cultural knowledge. It will show the extent to which the affecting presence has been subjected to critical examination and analysis; and this information alone, quite apart from the actual facts such analysis reveals about the affecting work in the particular culture, is itself further revealing of the intellectual habits of the people.

The study of the physical object that is often near-sightedly confounded with the affecting presence is little pursued. By "physical study" I mean the complete description of the physical properties of a work, and indeed of a wide range of works in one form, toward the end of reaching such generalizations as one can about the physical demeanor of the affecting work in a culture. Generalizations that are reached through such a study would differ from those formulated by means of a proper and relevant study of the affecting presence *qua* affecting presence in the respect that they would concern themselves solely with those analytical or descriptive concepts proper to the notation, enumeration, and measurement of the physical properties of the media.

Music, dance, and verse are alone the forms advantaged by a system of notation which relatively clearly reveals some of their physical properties. In all three forms, the duration of constituent parts is shown—by means of various temporal devices in music and dance, by line length in verse; stress is indicated in musical notation and is easily possible in verse, as Gerard Manley Hopkins has demonstrated; tone is easily indicated in both systems—and so on. This is a situation which contrasts markedly with that of narrative, where the system of notation

[4] See page 188 for the special sense in which this word is used.

reveals little of the physical properties of the work. Sculpture, painting, and costume do not of course enjoy a system of notation owing to the unique perpetration of each work in these forms.

A further property of the physical work is its structure, which incorporates the interrelationships that exist among all the features of the properties of one medium, as indeed it does among all the properties of all the constituent media of the work. The unique property of structure is *relationality,* and aside from the relations of *before* and *after,* and certain elements of dynamics in each of the three forms for which revealing notation exists, relationality is not indicated. Indeed, the question of relationality in the physical works has been given meager attention.

In any event, the physical study of the work should be pursued —its problems defined, its analysis effected, its anthropological promise perceived. But before this can be done, it is of the greatest urgency to establish a highly generalized language capable of identifying and describing constituent physical units and of stating their relationships. Until this is done, one cannot reach the point where he can speak with complete authority on the affecting forms in culture. The establishment of common terms from the examination of many such forms in many different cultures is essential if one is to be able to speak of the affecting presence in general and to derive a set of descriptive and analytical concepts and statements that will facilitate cross-cultural studies.

Thus, all the media want a meta-language such as exists for linguistics. Narrative is a case in point. The content analyst can discern units of narrative but has not done much work in the area of developing a vocabulary to express the relationships among those parts; indeed neither he nor the literary critic has studied the kinds of affecting relationships which may obtain. The situation is the same for the other forms as well. One can transcribe all the colors, volumes, notes, or movements that occur, but is this not merely at the level equivalent to phonetics? Where are the "phonemes" and the "syntagmemes"? Are "before and after" and "adjacent, above, beyond, within, and below" the only relationships of properties in time and space? What we face is the necessity of exploring the space and time in which the affecting presence exists, with the objective of ascertaining the "logic" of relationships.

42

The Study of the
Affecting Presence

The physical and social study of the affecting presence rests upon a view of culture which acknowledges that it is composed of both physical and mental phenomena. But there is a third component of human culture, the affective; it is a powerful domain which includes felt values, dreams, affecting symbols, natural objects and events to which affect has accrued, and the affecting presence. The affective realm is the universe of man's interiority, and its mode of address is direct. As with the physical and mental areas of culture, it is characterized not only by universals but also by both cultural and idiosyncratic modifications of those universals. Thus the experience of love, hate, loyalty, fear, and other such emotions is universal, but the circumstances under which these emotions are characteristically generated and the means of their expression are subject to cultural variables, while subscription to these norms and the intensity of feeling is obviously subject to individual variability. We have already seen something of the culturality of emotion in the example of the collision of Javanese bicycle riders.

Because the nature of the affective life is basic and because like physical and mental culture it has its own forms, this book is addressed to the proposition that the only meaningful apperception, description, and study of the affecting presence is in terms related to affect. Affect is the interior condition of feeling relating to the presence or absence of socially articulated values,

43

or to the presence of felt, "visceral" values. An affecting presence results only when its initiator is value-involved and when the values which move him are immediately presentable (not *representable*) in the nine media. The Statue of Liberty, for example, was intended to incarnate majesty, towering strength, gigantic capacity—all of which were then contemporary ideas about America, and it was possible to present them as well as the sculptor's feelings about them in a work. On the other hand, it is not possible to make a similar kind of statement about the marvelous forms of Brancusi; rather, the value in the instance of "The Kiss" is related to the "goodness" of the form itself—the sculptural volumes and their interrelationships constitute a positive value in their own terms and for the work's own sake. There is, finally, the instance in which a representational work assumes an added value—that accruing to it by virtue of the perceptor's attitude toward the external "model." But this is clearly extrinsic to the affecting presence and, as such, of no relevance to us here. The perception of the affecting presence must rest upon the recognition of felt or articulated values, and upon the power of the media and form; its study must proceed—from the universal, cultural, historical, and individual dimensions of such values, media, and forms.

As there are fundamental logical structures underlying man's rational activities,[1] such that all men reason from cause to effect and from effect to cause, irrespective of the reliability or the empirical factuality of their data, so may we assume that there is a basic substratum of identity to the content and mode of operation of man's affective life. All men love good and eschew evil, are awed by or are contemptuous of power, seek pleasure and—as far as they can—avoid pain; they are solicitous of those they love, penalize wrong-doers, pay respect to or shrink in fear from the powerful, and reward those who provide them with pleasure. This by no means, of course, represents the gamut of values and how they operate; but however defined, these are true of all men. This is the world of affect, and the feelings of this world are the powers that inform the affecting presence. All men thus have *in potentia* the receptivity for the affecting works of all other men, even though encountering an exotic affecting presence is sometimes like hearing two men speaking earnestly in a foreign

[1] See the works of Lucien Lévy-Bruhl.

44

tongue—one may not know precisely what is being said, but he can be aware of the presence of seriousness and be respectful of the fact that meaning of some grave sort is embodied in their encounter.

In view of the existence of cultural and individual factors defining the circumstances and the expression of basic human emotions, it is the task of the anthropologist, working with discrete instances of human actions in exotic cultures, to try to illuminate them for us not only in terms of their location and significance in the social structure and the political organization but also in terms of their import in interiority, their reality-in-being to those who feel—an illumination in terms of what the people feel as well as in terms of what they do. It is this kind of a goal that ennobles anthropology and makes it a discipline far more humane, more discriminating, and more relevant to the total human condition than it presently is. It is this kind of information which the anthropologist must provide if we are to advance toward an appropriate apperception of the exotic affecting presence. On the other hand, it is probable that the anthropologist must be guided by the humanist in the use of those highly developed sensitivities to things affecting that have traditionally characterized the best humanistic studies of man's affecting works. The humanist—freeing the anthropologist from the limiting, partialistic, and mechanistic view which has held him in bondage—can lead the anthropologist to a fuller and thus a truer account of man.

But often, to be sure, the humanist can be as reprehensible—and, needless to say, as wrong—as any anthropologist, for whereas the latter may not take account of the whole man, the humanist may also err by failing to take into account the importance of cultural or historical variables. The understanding of the affecting presence must rest upon a knowledge of the particular cultural world within which the affecting presence was created to live. There are few critics who would write an essay on *Moby Dick* without a thorough understanding of necessitarianism and a close familiarity with whaling, with Melville's times, and even with his own personal library. Serious people do, however, think to write about the novels of Chinua Achebe without any knowledge whatsoever of Ibo culture, and certainly nothing of the circumstances, the postures, or the intensities of Ibo feelings. Such critics make the most elementary kind of mistake, that of

45

assuming two things to be identical because they share certain superficial characteristics. It is not simply that the physical and cultural life in Achebe's works differs from ours as much as—or more than—life in the works of Melville differs from our world today, but more that one must ascertain the enormously important contours and content of a different system of affect which constitutes the existential field within which the affecting presence is created and endures.

As I have indicated, most operations performed upon the physical and social facets of the affecting presence are irrelevant to the study of the work *qua* affecting presence. This judgment is meant to include those studies which are devoted to the subject matter, or even those devoted to analysis of primary, affecting media of the works—such as a study of alliteration in the sonnets of Shakespeare—because they are not executed in terms which are directly related to the work's affecting existence. If we are always aware that the use of affecting media is inevitably of some degree of affecting reality, even if we cannot through interrogation indubitably attribute the proper feeling, we can perhaps in the long run ourselves begin to get a feeling of the import of the works. It is essential to realize that with respect to a given category of feeling, a work or a feature of a work can be more or less affective.

Not only may the physical features of the affecting presence be more or less affecting, some of them may not be affecting at all. If they are affecting, they may be said to be "distinctive," and they are so according to a criterion as simple and as uncompromising—if not perhaps as sharply defined—as that of the linguist who asserts that if a new sound feature makes for a new meaning, then that sound feature is distinctive. Thus there is no difference in English between *kot* and *kot'* but there is between *kot* and *kod;* 'd' and 't' are phonemic, but whether one aspirates after a final 't' in *cot* is not of significant difference. More elegantly, one can say that in this instance, voicing (the difference between 't' and 'd') is significant but aspiration is not. Significant physical features in the affecting presence, analogously, are feeling-related. If it is affectingly irrelevant whether a line is so long or a bit longer, or whether a passage of music is crisply executed, these factors are not distinctive. They are distinctive—or significant—on the other hand, if such variations have discernible affecting consequence. In sum, the affecting presence, just

46

as words, may be characterized by both accidental and distinctive features.

The relevant study of the affecting presence must be based upon this knowledge that all of its physical aspects are not equally important, that some are more or less affecting, and that some indeed may even be accidental, or extrinsic to the affecting totality. Such a study may proceed only in the terms provided by the most thoughtful analysis of the human circumstances and the emotional context of the work's existence. In many instances, since it is so difficult—if not indeed impossible—to elicit from informants the requisite data of interiority, the existence of affecting power or whether a feature is more or less affecting (though not the category and precise nature of the feeling itself) will have to be inferred from close observation and from a systematic and imaginative analysis of the use of the affecting media and of their enactment and their discipline in the various forms. Indeed, the study of the media and the forms of the affecting works of the Yoruba of Nigeria, to which we shall presently come, while by no means related to the address of *particular* values or feelings, is an instance of the use of just such a procedure—reasoning *from* recurring instances of identical treatment of the various media *to* the inference that these recurring phenomena assert common, though unidentified, conditions of being or existence in feeling.

The study of the physical properties of one or more affecting works is *aesthetics*. The enlargement of the study to include all instances of a given form (sculpture, for instance)—or as many as possible—for the purpose of discerning that which is generic and distinctive as opposed to that which is particular and/or accidental, makes the study one of *aesthemics*. Finally, when one's purpose is to ascertain those aesthemic properties which are common to all media in all forms, *mutatis mutandis,* then one is concerned with *para-aesthemics*—whether his interests extend over the affecting presences of a culture or of a culture area.

In an earlier essay,[2] I made a further point, namely that we may call the study of the interior half of the affecting-presence-in-transaction *pathetics* when the concern is with the responses to

[2] See my chapter, "The Arts in Human Culture: Their Significance and Their Study," in *Expanding Horizons in African Studies,* ed. Gwendolen Carter (Evanston: Northwestern University Press, 1969).

an individual work, and *pathemics* when our field of study is a form and our problem the identification of those least common denominators of feeling that define and quicken the aesthemes. Since there is in every pathetic response that which is idiosyncratic as well as that which is cultural, we may most usefully regard the patheme at a cultural level, omitting the idiosyncratic. Thus the basic feeling characteristically experienced in a given culture in response to a given aestheme is its patheme. *Parapathemics* is the term to use if the study is of the pathemics of all forms, in an attempt to come to an understanding of the content, boundaries, and media-relatedness of the feelings—all this at the level of culture or culture area.

But the question must be raised whether in fact one can separate experienced affect (pathetics) from those physical features which, in any given case of affecting-presence-in-transaction, are equal and sufficient presentations of such feelings. The conclusion I fear must be that it cannot, for to distinguish between aesthetics and pathetics is to fall prey to the materialism of the most ardent and unregenerate behaviorists, the simplistic antiphony of inevitably bipartite processes, such as stimulus-response. But most importantly, this dichotomy must be rejected simply because it is a dichotomy, because it suggests that very distinction between form and meaning which I have maintained is untrue of the affecting presence, but true—or relatively more true, at least—of the symbol.

The enactment, the incarnation which is the affecting presence, is directly perceived as and for what it is, and what it *is* is inextricably affecting. A line, a form, a work has its "significance," to be sure, but not in some mythical, "pathetic" realm; significance rather lies in the fact that a line or a tone or a volume is an indispensable element in the *achievement of the being* of the work. Thus is an affecting work presentational. Its particular presenceness is immediately presented to us. The "meaning" of the affecting presence is its existence and it is its existence which is apperceived and feelingfully acknowledged in the terms it demands—those very terms of its existence.

I have already discussed the physical properties of the affecting presence under the topics of their constitutive media and their forms. (See pp. 15–19.) Now, however, I shall carry this a step

8. *Leather Wayang puppet, Jogjakarta.*

further and mention the affecting-physical properties of the whole—the affecting style, affecting structure, affecting finish, affecting substance, affecting content, affecting virtuosity, and affecting dynamics. In each instance, as the use of the attributive "affecting" is intended to indicate, the property that is of concern is that which is distinctive rather than that which is accidental. Distinctiveness is determined by affecting significance, and this is to be perceived in two ways—by means of the interrogation of informants and by means of the careful analysis of works. Since our knowledge of the affecting is slight, let us work with the level at which it undeniably exists—the totality, where the *affecting* is perceived as a *gestalt*. At this level, particularly culturally (para-aesthemically), one will most profitably search for configurations of these affecting properties of the whole, configurations which hold true, to one degree or another, *mutatis mutandis,* for each of the forms in the culture. What is the significance for the phenomena under study of the view I have proposed of the affecting work as presence rather than symbol? It lies in this—that it is only in terms of this organic view that the systemic nature of the forms is explained. There is no *necessity* for the forms of symbols which would explain these systemic identities.

These several affecting features of the affecting presence, unlike the simple media which constitute them, are composite, involving as they do relationships among features of different media, or disciplines of media, or relationships among more than one instance of features of the same medium, and attendant disciplines—or, indeed, simultaneously involving both of these kinds of compositeness. This will become clear as we discuss each of them in turn.

Affecting Structure

The ensemble, temporal, or spatial array of all properties of media or of all parts of the affecting presence quite obviously is the structure of the affecting presence. If one seeks to determine that array of *distinctive features,* he strives to disclose the affecting structure of the work. Structure can also be that array constituted by the interrelationships of the various structured media composing the form. Thus in sculpture, which is composed of situationality, volume, relationality, surface, experience, and sometimes color and movement, one may seek to disclose

the inferred aesthetic or aesthemic structure of volume by perceiving and stating the relationships among such volumes, or
may quite as relevantly state the relationships among all the
media, either in total inventory of physical features or in respect
of distinctive media features. The same is true of dance, graphics,
music, architecture, drama, verbal narrative, and poetry, each
in terms of its own constitutive media. Structure is composite in
each of the three senses following, for it involves the relationships among features of different media, relationships among
features in the same medium, and, therefore, both. Furthermore,
these relationships may be either synchronic or diachronic, and
either of media in the same, successive, or adjacent spaces or
moments.

Affecting Style

The characteristic fashion in which structure is wrought, either
cultural or idiosyncratic, the way in which the media are disciplined in the forms, is that aspect of the affecting presence
which is termed style, a term which is recurringly subjected to
the broadest imaginable range of uses. As we shall have the
occasion to see later, style may be viewed in terms of a markedly
economical system of opposites—two, in fact: whether the treatment of features stresses *extension* in space or in synchronicity,
or in contrast, rigorous *intension*.[3] Extension/intension are to
be regarded as disciplines of the media. Style may thus be seen
to be a composite of media and their structures, *in terms of* the
discipline to which those media and structures are characteristically subjected in enactment. Style is further to be characterized in terms of whether the axis of the work asserts a *continuity* or, contrariwise, a *discontinuity* of development. Style
is affecting when it can be asserted that it is integral to the presentational being of the work.

Affecting Finish

Obviously, affecting finish by its very nature does not involve
structure, which must be conceived of as organic. This is true
even though structure may be traced or emphasized by details

[3] The reader should not confuse *intension*, as contrasted with *extension*, with *intention*.

of finish. Finish is a composite of media and of the discipline of those media, and it exists as adjunctive elements or patterns. Such features are of course distinctive (as is the case in all these properties) when they are in themselves affecting. Decoration is one form of adjunctive property of the finish—no matter in what form—as is the association of features which, resident in finish, tends to increase the affect of a piece, such as, for example, the patina of smoke and sacrificial blood that lends awe to the Night Society masks of the Bangwa.

Affecting Substance

Substance is a composite of media, affecting style, affecting surface and "what-ness" of the work, toward the end of presenting the subject matter of the affecting presence. As such it is superordinate to *structure,* as it is also to *style* and to *finish,* although it is subordinate to *content.* One's view of the media, under the model of substance, is not of the relationships of media components but rather of their service to the ends of achieving the presentation. This is an achievement made possible through the existence of a complicated structure of *metaphors,* those processes and conventions by means of which we are able to create affecting presences rather than merely signs or symbols or serviceable items. Substance thus is not just the media but the relationships between the media and the subject or the intention of the work, for the intention of the affecting presence is intrinsic to the work and not extrinsic to it as is the case in the symbol. Substance is the media-contained, total factualization of the affecting presence.

Affecting Content

Substance as just defined would seem to be all-inclusive, defined as the total factualization of the affecting presence, the successful incarnation of the essential intention of the work. But yet there is something more, the affective context within which the work must exist, a context composed of attendant and related feelings which, cultural or idiosyncratic, inevitably enrich the substance. Both affecting substance and affecting content together constitute the *presentation* of the affecting presence.

9. *Wood Wayang puppet, Jogjakarta.*

Affecting Virtuosity

A state of gratifying, indeed affecting, excellence and mastery of structure, style, finish, substance, and content is virtuosity. In one sense it is erroneously included here, for it is a condition of the other composite properties rather than a composite itself. But virtuosity is a special affecting property of the affecting presence and is one whose nearly universal reality causes all people to place special value upon some works in contrast to most others.

Affecting Dynamics

The masterful control of affecting dynamics is a cardinal feature in the achievement of virtuosity. This is the control of all of the foregoing affecting-physical properties of the whole—their balance, juxtaposition, contrast, repetition, variation, and rhythm.

54

The Affecting Presence
and Metaphor

A symbol and an affecting presence differ one from the other in that the former represents while bearing no necessary physical similarity to what it represents, except perhaps in certain instances of onomatopoeia, whereas the affecting presence presents and is physically identical to what it presents and is—by metaphor—also identical to the emotion which is transferred in the affecting transaction.

If we hear a musical composition which is lyrical, slow, and in a minor key, we are likely to feel a sweet anguish and sorrow not because those features refer to such an emotional state, but because they indeed constitute the external dimensions, indeed equivalents, of that estate, inevitably invoking it in the sensitive and appropriately culture-imbued perceptor. This is owing to the operation of the complex process of metaphorization which, as symbolization is the process of externalizing or projecting reason, is the method by which feeling is made incarnate in works—affecting presences—which are themselves presentations but not, of course, perceptors of emotions.

A symbol mediates between the intention or projection of meaning and its comprehension. A metaphor, which makes intention inherent in the work, is not a process of mediation but of immediation. If "presentation" bespeaks the sense of being that characterizes the affecting presence—its intention-content-transacting totality—"immediation" is intended to denote the self-sufficiency of the agents in the affecting transaction. By this I mean that both the work and its perceptor are self-existent. They encounter, transact, and then the act of perception, the experience of encounter, is terminated; and the perceptor, if the transaction has indeed occurred, grows with respect to the work and under the precise conditions of the work, much as he does after an encounter with a person who has instantly created an impact within him.

Despite the essential difference between the processes of externalizing the content of the mind and of the spirit, symbolization and metaphorization are nonetheless otherwise comparable processes as their dynamics of being involve relationships of unlikes—sound and meaning in one instance, form and feeling in the other. Since actual objects cannot be manipulated within the head, phonetic events take their places and the objective world is made manageable. The inner world presents different problems, however. If I say I am feeling sad, I am naming how I feel but not in fact presenting my feeling. By means of words, I can no more bring out into the open that precise mood which is my sadness than I can produce an object to which I have referred, say the Golden Gate bridge. I can do this only if I leave the universe of symbols and enter into that world uniquely constituted to "immediate" what I feel, both to myself as well as to another perceptor, for creator is always perceptor to his own work. As is the case with the mediation of symbols, this immediation comes into being not by virtue of my actual feeling of sadness, which is after all only mine, but rather by material means in point of sheer physical composition quite unlike my sadness in essence. The material features are nonetheless amenable to being forged into combinations, ultimately into forms, which will finally constitute, in their own terms, my sadness—a feeling which when externalized is no longer mine but in fact becomes its own, its self. Such a work will immediate a particular sadness, as particular as it is within the skills at my command to effectuate. The process of metaphorization is infinitely particular.

Metaphor is as inalienable a fact of human existence as is the symbol. Its materials are the affecting media on the one hand, disciplined by the affecting features on the other hand, to the end that an affecting presence results. This is truly one of the most elementary and astounding magics of human existence. How-

56

ever this miraculous process unites unlikes making likes of them, it seems safe to presume that it is a process whose beginnings rest on the premise that representation or imitation of a thing or an event in a medium different from the original thing or event is possible. From that simple and self-evident fact the magic takes over, such that representation itself becomes no longer the item of chief interest, for the work begins to assume an identity and a life of its own. The work begins to become an affecting presence and to assert its own value—its own being—in its own terms, over and above—and different from—the original

Table 2. Metaphorical Bases of the Forms

FORMAL METAPHORS

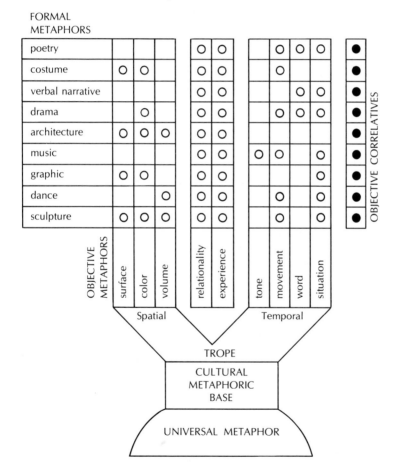

FORMAL METAPHORS	surface	color	volume	relationality	experience	tone	movement	word	situation	OBJECTIVE CORRELATIVES
poetry				O	O	O	O	O		●
costume	O	O		O	O	O				●
verbal narrative				O	O		O	O		●
drama		O		O	O	O	O	O		●
architecture	O	O	O	O	O					●
music				O	O	O	O		O	●
graphic	O	O		O	O				O	●
dance			O	O	O		O		O	●
sculpture	O	O	O	O	O		O		O	●

OBJECTIVE METAPHORS — Spatial | Temporal

TROPE

CULTURAL METAPHORIC BASE

UNIVERSAL METAPHOR

57

model. As I have pointed out previously, it is treated as a being. From its birth in the possibilities of representation, the affecting presence springs into being, often, as we know, by virtue of metaphors which provide no suggestion that representation is in the slightest the incarnate intention.

The force of being which characterizes the affecting presence derives from the tension existing among the media and their properties at one level, and at another level among the affecting features of the whole (finish, substance, etc.) and intentionality, as well indeed as between the two levels. Philip Wheelwright has drawn attention to tension as the basic dynamic of metaphor, thus initiating my thinking on this point,[1] and his discussion is therefore basic to this present analysis. He has perceived clearly that it is the structure of tensions which asserts the energy characteristic of that marvelous entity which is the affecting presence.

Metaphor, as a fundamental human property, exists as a complex system extending through levels or orders from particular works back to a universal metaphor which is rooted in the nature of the human psyche, as deeply and as surely as is the pattern which causes humans to analyze their world into concepts, actors, actions, and attributes, ultimately to burgeon forth with numerous languages, each with its infinite possibilities of particular utterances. In any given culture, the relations among these various levels of metaphor are such that they may be said to have genetic relationships, with every subsequent level depending upon and indeed including every prior one. In order to reveal the contours of this system, I shall present it level by level, commencing with the most familiar one, the particular affecting presence.

Objective Correlative

For the name of the metaphoric level represented by the individual affecting presence, I have chosen T. S. Eliot's term *objective correlative*, although I naturally do not intend that it designate a process characteristic solely of literature. In perceiving that a given image constituted the objective correlative of an emotion, Eliot went straight to the heart of metaphor as

[1] Philip Wheelwright, *Burning Fountain: A Study in the Language of Symbolism*, rev. ed. (Bloomington: Indiana University Press, 1968).

58

it operates in particular instances. It is precisely this same kind of phenomenon which is at work in the other forms as well, a constellation of media and media properties, assuming form and affecting features, and constituting, either in part of the work or in the work's totality, the objective correlatives of particular emotions or sets of emotions. Sculptural volumes, tonal qualities, surface and color, balletic movement—all these are exploited to the ends of achieving feeling by virtue of working and annealing them into affecting works. In each medium, therefore, and in every form, the phenomenon of the objective correlative is to be found. And since there is more than one affective state to be achieved, there is a multiplicity of objective correlatives; clusters of them are responsive to or evocative of different classes of feelings, with the whole corpus constituting a "lexicon" of objective correlatives. Milton's "L'Allegro" and "Il Penseroso" are examples of two such items, neatly differentiated from one another, clearly separate "terms" in the "lexicon," as indeed are any two similarly contrasting musical compositions— Haydn's "Surprise Symphony" and Sibelius' "Valse Triste"—two paintings, two sculptures, or two ballets, or any separably meaningful parts thereof.

Similetic Metaphor

It goes without saying that "terms" which respond to or initiate the same category of affect may be regarded in this respect as "synonyms" to one another. Not only are two "happy" poems synonymous with respect to the feeling of happiness, but a happy poem, a happy musical composition, and a happy painting are also all synonyms. Synonymity thus obtains not only within but also across forms. But the precise nature of synonymity remains to be determined.

There is but one sensibility and it operates through the senses, the doors to the feelings in their capacity as the dynamic functions of the sensibility. Using the concept of pity as an example, one may thus make either of two assumptions: there may be a distinct category of pity responsive to the appropriate affecting stimuli in each of the forms, or there may be one category of such feeling identically responded to by the appropriate affecting presence regardless of the form. The former posits multiple categories of one feeling (pity via sculpture, pity via

59

music, etc.), while the latter assumes but one. Obviously it is simpler and more elegant to make the second of these assumptions and once having made it, a significant conclusion follows: all affecting presences responsive to or initiative of a common feeling, irrespective of the physical differences of various forms, are equivalent to one another, and the physical structures or features in the various forms that bring about such identities of feeling are, *mutatis mutandis,* equivalent para-aesthemic structures or features.

With due caution one may turn this argument about so that, lacking certain knowledge about the nature or content of the affective response, the worker, perceiving what he believes to be a significant constellation of physical properties, can assume that it has an affective consequence and that it has equivalents in the other media. Granting that with respect to a given feeling each of the forms bears an identical relationship to the sensibility, the detective work of finding equivalents is simply that. Thus it is clear that in terms of the metaphoric process, "Il Penseroso" and "Valse Triste" are affectively synonymous and are objective correlatives of roughly the same category of feeling.

As the metaphoric process operates in the first place to make it possible through a system of conventions to objectify the correlative of an emotion in a medium which cannot have any common physical features with that emotion, so does the metaphoric process operate to elect certain characteristics in each of the forms as being equivalent to one another with respect to the creation of an objective correlative of a given feeling in any and all forms. That facet of the metaphoric process which asserts that, for the purpose of achieving a common affective end, a given way of treating certain physical characteristics in one form will be equal to a certain other way of treating the same physical characteristics in another form may be called the process of the similetic metaphor.

The similetic metaphor, although treated here at the level of the objective correlative, must be seen as obtaining at each level in the analysis thus far described as well as among those orders of the metaphoric system I shall hereafter designate as *formal metaphor, objective metaphor,* and *trope.* The similetic metaphor exists not only among forms, but among the media and their properties as well.

60

10. *Terra cotta head, Nok.*

I am definitely not asserting a case of point-by-point identity, of absolute and total equivalence among different works in various media which are productive of common kinds of affect. I must stress the fact that they are *roughly* equivalent or, rather, broadly defined with respect to the emotional target area. I have asserted that the process of metaphorization is an exercise in uniqueness, and given this fact, one cannot logically assert absolute equivalence among works. The process of making works unique cannot be denied even in those cases where all works constitute a class of presumably identical (with respect to function) works—such as the twin figures among the Yoruba. For their ritualistic identity notwithstanding—and this dimension of the work's existence is as secondary and external a nature to the work as affecting presence as is the act of reference to a portrait—each ibeji is in fact its own work. Thus it is that in some more highly generalized sense, certain works or features may be seen as the equivalents of one another.

Formal Metaphor

Antecedent to the objective correlative is the formal metaphor, which is the level of the forms—sculpture, music, architecture, dance, poetry, verbal narrative, costume, and dream. These forms obviously do not constitute the objective correlatives of particular emotions, but together they account for the total inventory of the affecting presences executed in all their variety in all the forms. It is at the level of the formal metaphor that the anthropologist works; for with respect to the affecting presence, the formal metaphor constitutes the level of observable culture, since it represents the highest possible order of generalization from the discrete instances of objective correlatives, i.e., the observable data.

Objective Metaphor

We have earlier discussed the fashion in which the forms are constituted through the exploitation of the properties of the various media and bound together into wholes by the special media of relationality and experience. The order of the objective metaphor is the level of the media and their properties, and it

11. *Terra cotta head, Nok.*

is metaphoric for precisely the same kinds of reasons that the other orders constitute levels of metaphor, that is to say that the phenomena at the level of objective metaphor have affecting consequence. To be sure, such consequences are not finely determined and discriminated; they cannot be, for such definition requires the available affecting resources of the media and their properties wrought in concert. It is axiomatic to assert that the greater the number of exploitable properties, the greater the degree of affecting definition.

Trope

Affecting presences can be created about one of three kinds of axes—spatial, temporal, and spatio-temporal. Sculpture and painting rely upon an axis of space; music, poetry, and narrative upon an axis of time; and costume, drama, and dance upon an axis of space-time. In resolving the question of how space, time, and space-time are transmuted via the objective metaphors into the affecting presence, we must pursue a line of reasoning similar to the one used under the discussion of the simile: either such transmutation is accomplished by one principle or by three separate ones. And once again elegance would dictate that we accept one principle as opposed to three. This principle must be neither spatial nor temporal but must be different from and anterior to both of them, yet construing both time and space systematically, for we have already seen that works responsive to a given feeling in one form or medium are, by virtue of the similetic metaphor, equivalent to works responsive to that same feeling in another form or medium. I assume thus that space and time respond to one master affective set or principle rather than to two entirely different ones—one set of feelings to be expressed in time and another to be expressed in space—and are therefore equivalent. This metaphoric order I call a *trope,* and the trope represents the bifurcation of far more basic metaphoric processes. The trope is also the most elementary order at which the similetic metaphor obtains. The trope itself is neither spatial nor temporal, but rather both. And so it tends to accept either time or space as its dominant mode of existence but subjects them both to a common metaphoric discipline.

64

Cultural Metaphoric Base

The trope dictates the terms of equivalence and establishes mode predominance in the space and time aspects of the metaphoric process. But there is yet another more basic level, antecedent to the trope, one which undergirds the whole metaphoric system, from objective correlatives to trope, and gives to the whole range of affecting presences of a given culture their cohesive, homogeneous cultural identity. At this level the metaphoric process, using the total range of the corpus of affecting presences irrespective of form, asserts something of affecting significance itself; it asserts the totality of style, the cultural identity, the historical reality of a people, and it perpetuates their feelings; even after the creators have disappeared from earth, like Ozymandias they confront us.

Romanticism is one such cultural metaphoric base, as are naturalism, realism, and what I have elsewhere called Guineaism.[2] Each of these cultural metaphoric bases can alter the culturally defined conventions which shape the whole system, down to the objective correlatives. They suffuse the affecting presence, the affecting system. There is every likelihood that as the cultural metaphoric base speaks through the affecting presence and the metaphoric system, so does it speak through the total affective life, giving a consistency of style to the ethos, touching not only sculpture, dance, music, painting, but food, clothing, fighting, house styles, interpersonal relations—all the soft, viable, fleshy, feeling parts of culture.

Universal Metaphor

Man has feelings; he expresses them, teaches them to others, and refines them through the agency of the affecting presence. We have discussed the role of metaphor at its various levels in making this possible. Anterior to the cultural metaphoric base is the irreducible universal metaphor which finds plastics malleable into forms; words and tones and events productive through imagination of delight as well as of information; and movement more gratifying—and different—in dance than it

---

[2] Robert P. Armstrong, "Guineaism," *Tri-Quarterly*, no. 5 (1966), pp. 137–46.

is in walking. Man has discovered that such delights express a third part of his being, and so he metaphorizes, creating affecting works. Can one reach universal generalizations about the means by which excitement is affectingly symbolized, or about anguish, or love? Can one assert anything meaningful about the affective dimension of the mere fact of existence that is universally true, or about a joyous metabolism, demonstrating its presentation in some basic and as of now unperceived aspect of the affecting presence? The answers to these questions must await the patient labors of years of careful, attentive, and imaginative research.

I have already described affecting style as the disciplining of the media in their forms into characteristic cultural or idiosyncratic configurations. From our discussions of metaphor, however, it is clear that what I have previously called affecting style is a function of the operation of the metaphoric system upon the media, and that style is therefore deeply pervasive of— indeed integral to and not decorative of or arbitrary to—the affective life of the culture, to an extent far greater than its name might indicate or the discussion of style as an affecting property of the work might initially suggest. Style is the visual evidence that the cultural metaphoric base exists, and even though one might have certain misgivings about using the term (which I shall nonetheless do), one can have no reservations about its being of adequate complexity, as already defined, to accommodate all the affectingly relevant phenomena of a certain sort which are resident in the disciplining of the media in a culturally or individually approved way.

All I have said of metaphor and affecting style is necessarily true as well for metaphor and affecting structure, for structure— as subordinate to style—is thus also genetically derivative from the metaphoric system. There is a difference, however: structure is expressive of all those affectingly relevant phenomena concerned not with the disciplining of the media with respect to extension/intension and continuity/discontinuity in space and time (which is style) but rather with those constitutive units of the work and with their interrelationships. If one speaks of the components of a work and their dynamics of relationship, he is speaking of structure. The characteristic structures of a people are to be seen as deeply and inescapably reflective of the cultural metaphoric base. So also are affecting substance, affecting content, affecting finish, and affecting dynamics. Viewed in terms of the system of metaphor, substance (which was earlier defined in other terms) is to be seen as a complex of metaphorically determined style, structure, finish, and dynamics under the sign of the work's "what-ness." Content is this same totality projected against the whole cultural spectrum of values. Finish is responsive to the metaphoric system as well, but its determinants are not those born of the organic intrusion of subject matter and values, but rather of the application of the nongenetic, the decorative—irrespective of how essential such finish may be conceived to be to the affecting presence.

Affecting structure and affecting style are disciplines exercised upon the affecting axes of works and thus are functions of time/space. Therefore they have their origin also in the cultural metaphoric base and find their expression in the trope.

Let us further consider the time/space trope. As we have just observed, it derives from the general affecting premise of the culture, and it must not only assert certain preferences about both extension and duration, but also must equate these preferences with values and with affective states. Thus all the parts (time/space, structure/style) are really assertions, albeit in different manners, of the identical affecting premise—let us say an overwhelming predilection to full, rounded development in all forms.

I have already defined style as involving the operation of either one of the two binomial elements in two pairs of opposites—extension and intension, and continuity and discontinuity—with respect to either space or time. Both space and time, however, are composed of parts, and it is of these parts only that extension and intension may be characteristic. This is to say that extension/intension characterize synchronic time and discrete space, even though they may, serially, suffuse the whole work. Adjacent spaces and diachronic time are subject to the disciplines of continuity and discontinuity. Similarly structure, as subordinate to style and as more particular, must involve the same binaries both synchronically and discretely, and diachronically and serially.

Let us say that a hypothetical culture prefers rounded, full-

67

bodied human relationships and asserts humanistic values. In its affecting works, it asserts the continuous and moderate extension. The continuous in both space and time is easily identifiable as that which projects through time and through space with minimal interruptions, for example those presentations of the body in sculpture in which the body most nearly attains the volume of a block or column. The closer a work approaches that presentation which gives the work the conformation of the natural body, the more it departs from continuity; and when that naturalistic mark is passed and the junctures of the body are stressed at the expense of the long lines, then discontinuity is approached. We may compare the figure of the Ibibio doll (fig. 7), which stresses continuity, with the Wayang leather puppet of Java (fig. 8), whose erratic bends and elaborate decorations deny the possibility of simple continuity and assert, in fact, discontinuity. As concerns time, the drive to follow through with emphasis upon the organic, diachronic development is continuity in time. On the other hand, the careful, simple, or elaborate definition of synchronic structures, with the frequent use of stop-time, asserts the exploitation of the principle of discontinuity.

We must assume, therefore, that our hypothetical culture, whose cultural metaphoric base asserts the affecting power of the continuous, will insofar as presentation is concerned execute structures that embody continuity. If, in portraiture, the model is itself given to minimally continuous volumes and times, idealization might occur (as happened in Greek as opposed to Roman portraiture) such that the most affectingly continuous execution possible will be made. We further expect that the temporal values will assert the flowing and the organic.

Extension/intension also exist on a continuum, from the maximally extended to that which is folded in upon itself. Extension is a property of limbs, features, and decorative elements, and thus as a result extension is largely a property of such attributes projecting into space. Extension can also be read as range, however; and that work which most exploits the possibilities of wide range is also characterized by extension. Intension is in all cases the opposite. Both extension and intension entail structural and stylistic consequences. Thus maximal extension tends to inhibit the development of strong continuity, as may be seen in the instance of a dancing Siva. Radical in-

69

Nomoli, Kissi.

tension, on the other hand, discourages the possibilities resident in the dramatic exploitation of juncture for dramatic effect. But irrespective of the structural consequences of either stylistic preference, the choice of intension versus extension is a variable independent of continuity versus discontinuity, as evidenced by the fact that either intensive or extensive continuity, and either intensive or extensive discontinuity may exist.

The trope thus brachiates the predispositions resident in the cultural metaphoric base into time/space, interpreted in the language of a style. Further, time arts with respect to the order of space derive a second order of spatiality via synchronic spread; space arts with respect to the order of time derive a second-order temporality via the exploitation of continuity and discontinuity. Thus, in the first instance, the variety of instruments and the range of tone simultaneously given in a chord of music, or of the configurations of bodies and dancers in an instant of time, if great are both analogous to spatial extension, or if restricted are both analogous to intension. In the second instance any point extended or repeated achieves second-order continuity or discontinuity. The double-outlined areas of Table 3 indicate the domains of second-order spatiality and temporality.

Table 3. Model: Continuity/Discontinuity and
Extension/Intension in Time and Space

	TIME	SPACE
CONTINUITY	through structure and organic development	genetic development of long surfaces and volumes
DISCONTINUITY	interruptions of time via stop-time, emphasis on synchronic structures	interruptions of planes and volumes, or multiple planes and volumes
EXTENSION	breadth of exploitation of features in synchronic structures	maximal reaching into space—centrifugality
INTENSION	inhibition of range of synchronic features	assertion of centripetality

Those means which achieve temporal and spatial continuity are by virtue of the similetic metaphor equivalents one of the other. So also are those which achieve temporal and spatial

13. *Head, Krinjabo, Anyi.*

discontinuity, temporal and spatial extension, and temporal and spatial intension.

Time, space, and time-space are, one or another of them, of necessity constant in the affecting presence, but the style and structure which actualize forms in time and space are variable and combinable. One may see this by arranging them to form a simple matrix:

Table 4. Model: Continuity/Discontinuity and
Intension/Extension as Matrix

	CONTINUITY	DISCONTINUITY
INTENSION		
EXTENSION		

This indicates that whether the form is spatial, temporal, or spatial-temporal, there exist four structural-stylistic possibilities: intensive continuity, intensive discontinuity, extensive continuity, and extensive discontinuity.

In terms of media, these structural-stylistic possibilities will have distinct characteristics which are suggested, necessarily briefly, in Tables 5 and 6.

This outline tallies all the alternative stylistic-structural situations possible in terms of the framework here developed. In order to extrapolate from this to the forms themselves, it is necessary only to refer to Table 1 to find the constitutive media of the forms, reading them from the appropriate structural-stylistic column.

Aesthemes are minimally those discrete physical conditions of the media which in a given culture are expressive of these four categories or modes of feeling and metaphor. Such aesthemes of media, whether *generally* or *particularly* expressive, are aesthemes of the part, and those principles of similetic equivalence which order a mode of feeling, or a particular feeling within the mode, are called para-aesthemes of the part. There is also to be considered, however, the work as a whole, as an assemblage of media. And there are aesthemic assemblages of such media, such that all media contribute toward the work's

72

Table 5. Model: Characteristics of Media in Intensive
Continuity/Discontinuity

	INTENSIVE CONTINUITY	INTENSIVE DISCONTINUITY
SURFACE	Emphasis on the linear and the dominant plane. Strong, simple quadrilateral or triangular areas.	Emphasis on juncture. Multiplicity of simple, quadrilateral or triangular areas.
VOLUME	Volumes as above.	Volumes as above.
COLOR	Narrow spectrum. Strong, simple color areas.	Narrow color spectrum. Multiplicity of color areas.
TONE	Narrow tonal spectrum. Diachronic density.	Narrow tonal spectrum. Synchronic emphasis. Much use of juncture.
MOVEMENT	Thrust with marked gathering of energies, a focused centrality of movement, with few interruptions. Stress on wholeness. Density of events in time.	Thrust with marked gathering of energies, a focused centrality, with structural units being truncated and many such units necessary to achieve desired end. Great use of juncture. Economy of events in time.
WORD	Establishment of rigorously minimal exploitation of properties in poetic continuum.	Establishment of rigorously minimal exploitation of poetic properties in succession of short units.
EXPERIENCE	Restricted inventory of experiential or experienced elements closely developed in continuum.	Restricted inventory of experiential or experienced elements in succession of incidents.
RELATIONALITY	Tightly woven relationships among large units expressing careful and long development.	Tightly woven relationships among short and dispersed units emphasizing shortness of affecting units.
SITUATION	Close control over complexity of situation with stress upon scrupulous genetic development.	Close control over complexity of situation with stress upon the synchronic and particular event at expense of genetic development.
	Similetic equivalents.	Similetic equivalents.

73

Table 6. Model: Characteristics of Media in
Extensive Continuity/Discontinuity

	EXTENSIVE CONTINUITY	EXTENSIVE DISCONTINUITY
SURFACE	Emphasis upon part extending into space, with the continuous emphasized.	Emphasis upon part extending into space at the expense of genetic relatedness.
VOLUME	Volumes as above.	Volumes as above.
COLOR	Broad color spectrum. Strong, simple color areas, genetically related.	Broad color spectrum. Multiplicity of small color areas, discrete and not genetically related.
TONE	Broad tonal spectrum. Diachronic density and relatedness.	Broad tonal spectrum. Synchronic emphasis. Much use of juncture. Weak genetic development.
MOVEMENT	A wide dispersion of directions of movement with radical economy of units. Stress on wholeness. Great range of events in both diachronic and synchronic phenomena. Density of genetically related diachronic events.	A wide dispersion of directions of movement with structural units truncated and multiple. Great range of events in both diachronic and synchronic phenomena. Development of events in synchronic order, use of stop-time, juncture, and a de-emphasis of genetic development.
WORD	Expanded exploitation of poetic properties in poetic continuum.	Expanded exploitation of poetic properties in succession of short poetic units.
EXPERIENCE	Expanded inventory of experiential or experienced elements developed in continuum.	Expanded inventory of experiential or experienced elements developed in succession of incidents.
RELATIONALITY	Extended or even loose relationships among large units expressing careful and long development.	Extended or even loose relationships among short and dispersed units emphasizing shortness of affecting units.
SITUATION	Emphasis upon complexity of situation with stress upon scrupulous genetic development.	Emphasis upon complexity of situation with stress upon the synchronic and particular event at expense of genetic development.
	Similetic equivalents.	Similetic equivalents.

74

total impact; these are aesthemes of the whole. These aesthemes of the whole, further, have equivalence both with respect to the mode and the particular feeling, and such equivalents are called para-aesthemes of the whole. It is these aesthemes of the whole which we markedly sense especially in the affecting works of an exotic culture, where we have little or no knowledge of particular affecting import.

I have already mentioned the act of reduction inherent in studying, and subsequently in talking or writing about, the affecting presence. This is in a sense true even when one is concerned solely and relevantly with the affecting presence in terms of its special affecting nature. The obvious reason behind this is that in so doing, one is inevitably translating from the affecting realm to the intellectual realm, and the two are separate universes of being. The affecting work does not exist relevantly outside of the presence of affect, and affect cannot be conveyed in reference-bound language—that is, it can be *denoted* but not *presented* discursively. One can cope adequately with affecting works only affectingly, because these various forms are not different "languages," as language itself is a different "language" from the affecting presence, but different "dialects" in the same "language," *the language of being.* The affecting presence exists and persists through the being-language of its "what-ness," its intention, its affecting media, its affecting properties, and its transactability, which assumes a position of subscribing to the translatability of the intentions of the affecting works from one form to another. Such a position inevitably follows from the systemic view developed here and particularly from the fact of similetic equivalence. Obviously there is room for considerable variability here. In the European works, where uniqueness is prized, point-to-point translatability is at best doubtful, for we have no precise notion of how finely aesthemes may be drawn. In the instance of the Yoruba, however, where more highly generalized works are created, the probability of translatability is very high indeed. In all cases, the aesthemes of the whole, as opposed to the aesthemes of the part, are translatable. It follows, then, that the only nonreductivistic way of coping with the affecting presence is in wholly affecting terms.

One sees the human constantly, though unconsciously, attest-

ing to the validity of this view in his uses of synaesthesia.[3] The constructs of synaesthesia are in fact cross-medial or cross-formal descriptions executed in the being-language, and their existence is possible, as well as their exploitation frequent, because of the wholeness of the realm of the affect and the economy of the metaphoric process which operates to define a cross-formal system of similetic equivalents. Synaesthesia is thus to be seen not as a rather marvelous, notable, and arbitrary invention. On the contrary, synaesthesia is an inevitable process, springing from an inalienable condition of man's being.

There are two views of synaesthesia: one sees the process as being constituted of confusions, a phenomenon which therefore has greatly interested certain psychologists, and another sees synaesthesia as a consciously exploited method of pinpointing reality. It is thus that it is used in the execution of affecting works. The trope itself, in which structure and style in spatial and temporal works are mutually translatable, is in all probability the fundamental basis of synaesthesia. Thus synaesthesia is to be seen at its base as a further and somewhat specialized extrapolation from the nature of the metaphoric process.

Alan Merriam, in *The Anthropology of Music,* employs the model of synaesthesia developed by the psychologists. That this should be the case is perfectly reasonable, consistent as it is with his behavioristic attitude toward "the arts." This view is not satisfactory to our argument here, however. It is the specific use of synaesthesia in the affecting presence which is most usefully of concern to these purposes. Glenn O'Malley surveys for us the distinction between the two concepts of synaesthesia.

> Miss [June] Downey's approach to the subject, though mainly a psychologist's, . . . [distinguishes] between "true" and literary (or "pseudo") synesthesiae. By true synesthesia she meant experience, not necessarily pathological, which leads a person to speak as though he has actually *heard* light or color *(audition colorée),* or *seen* sounds (tonal vision). Literary synesthesia, as investigations into imagery of Keats, Poe, Swinburne, and others convinced her, did not necessarily reflect confusions at the sensory level (and in all likelihood rarely reflected any) but was primarily imaginative exploitation of assumptions

---

[3] For two excellent discussions of synaesthesia, see Alan P. Merriam, *The Anthropology of Music* (Evanston: Northwestern University Press, 1964), and Glenn O'Malley, *Shelley and Synesthesia* (Evanston: Northwestern University Press, 1964).

77

Head, Ife, Yoruba.

that data of one sense could somehow resemble those of another. . . . For intelligent study of intersense analogies in literature her distinction between "spontaneous" (true) and "deliberate" (literary) comparisons marked a great advance. . . .[4]

It is this deliberate synaesthesia, used to develop and define the important particularities of the affecting presence, that is of interest to us here.

The question is whether the phenomena of synaesthesia are properly to be thought of as being "intersense analogies" (Merriam calls synaesthesia "intersense modalities"). It is true that they are perceived and construed in terms of the senses—how else can they be? Otherwise they would be finely drawn ideas. But the question is whether they are addressed to the content of the senses and to the act of sensing or, rather, to what the content of the senses and sensing, under very particular circumstances, is addressed to. It seems to me very clear that the address is to the latter, since the senses as such are activated only by direct stimuli of specific physical characteristics. When one speaks of a "strident color," the color is not in fact characterized by those features of sound which constitute stridency. One says rather that in respect to that affect which stridency produces, the color in question has affecting features which are identical to the affecting features of stridency. "Intersense analogy" is thus a misleading term, for it is not intersense but rather intermedia, since the affecting media are the stuff of the affecting presence.

"Analogy" does appear to suggest the proper model for what in fact occurs. With respect to "strident color," one is not, it seems to me, saying that "this color is to color in general (or other instances of the particular color) as stridency is to sound." One is maintaining rather that "this color is to my sensibility, to my response in transaction, as stridency of sound is to my response to such a sound in transaction." Once again, it is affect and not sense per se which is the relevant consideration. Locke's blind man in *Essay Concerning Human Understanding*, having never seen scarlet, correctly judged its affecting nature without sense stimulus of scarlet—he inferred that it was like a trumpet.

The intention of synaesthesia is not to communicate to the reason—not to build a novel referent to a symbol—nor to simu-

---

[4] O'Malley, *Shelley and Synesthesia*, pp. 5–6.

late a particular sensation for the senses to enjoy, but rather to present by creation that which is affectingly real. Synaesthesia is an intermedial drama which establishes and illuminates a new reality; it is a dialectic in the language of being whose synthesis is the novel in experience.

Method

Traditionally, the affecting presence has been studied for a variety of reasons. It has been examined for the light it can throw upon various aspects of social or economic life, for what it shows us about its own historical period, to document that a given personage was at a given time in Verona and not in Rome, for example, and to trace the spread of a technique or an ideological movement. Such studies are eminently justifiable, but to assume that they are studies of the affecting presence is to make a gratuitous and erroneous assumption. These are no more studies of the affecting work than a study of social history, or institutions, or of the lives of great men who sat for portraits is the proper, relevant study of the affecting work. This is not to say that history, great men, important institutions, and even the creators themselves are without relevance to the study of the affecting presence. Indeed any area which expands awareness of factors which have experiential and affecting significance will help illuminate the nature of the experience incarnate in the work, restoring to it—if it is a work from an exotic culture or an alien time—something of its native reality.

I do not mean to suggest that all study of the affecting presence has been irrelevant, for that would be absurd, although most social scientists' studies may be so characterized. But the works of great aestheticians and art historians have seldom failed to come to grips with the affecting work in its proper terms, irre-

80

spective of their final view concerning the ontology of the work. The best of such men have always illuminated affecting works with the age in which they appeared—and in turn brought the age to life with the works; but they have not debased the work by failing to treat it as what it is, as consistent with its own nature, as a vital presence in itself. They have achieved their ends by being ever mindful of the affecting presence, by searching out the factors in its dynamic balance among intention, the affecting media and their properties, and the affecting features them-selves—the work, on the one hand, and the perceptor in trans-action, on the other.

Something about the affecting presence causes the perceptor to say of it that it is *good* or *bad*. He is not content merely to enter into transaction with the work; he must evaluate it—quite as he does another man—in terms of what he conceives to be the intent and the success of its being; and "good" and "bad" are the prime terms in the lexicon of evaluation, whether of the human being or of the affecting work. We should note in passing that these terms are not always used solely with reference to the work itself and to its ability to satisfy in its own terms; on the contrary, in some instances "good" and "bad" are taken to refer only to the moral idea inherent in or some of the superficial moral attitudes characteristic of the substance of the work. In such a case the work is presumed to be even more closely akin to the human being, for it is made to bear the penalties of "wrong thinking" and is accordingly proscribed or destroyed. Evaluation, however much it may be a seemingly natural accompaniment of encounter with the affecting presence, should not be the con-cern of the social scientist in his dealing with affecting works, at this stage at least, especially if those works should have their origin in an exotic culture. Approaching the understanding of the work is the first step, without seeking to leap to that sense of virtuosic intimacy which makes judgment possible.

The affecting presence is the human act perpetually in action so that others, including its own creator, might subsequently come to experience it. It can only be understood in its own terms as there are no others, since it does not have meaning but has only being. It is possible to study the affecting work as being in its own terms. But this is the "study" of direct experience; it is the way the mystic studies God. Indeed from one point of view this is all that is possible. But we are accustomed to under-

81

15. *Head, Ife, Yoruba.*

standing by "study" that process of inquiry which produces an order of "factuality," amenable to being conveyed from one person to another by words discursively employed.

We assume, therefore, that the affecting presence can be studied and communicated about, however unsatisfactorily, and that discourse concerning it will involve reductions which, though being simplistic and existing in a different universe, are nonetheless more relevant to the work than certain other reductions might be. We also assume that because the world of the affect is common to all men and because of the existence of the universal metaphor, any worker from any culture is bound to experience a basic substratum of rapport with the affecting presence of any culture. The practical significance of this is that if the student will persist in his determination to study the affecting presence in its own terms, unless he is totally without sensitivity to the affecting universe and to the nature of metaphor, he will share with the creator at least some of the basic points of departure. If he is to study the works of an exotic culture, and it is mostly such a person with whom I am here concerned, his inferences must be in the direction of apperceiving the cultural metaphoric base, for it is here that the generalizations reside which in subsequent refinement and specialization accomplish all the particular affecting eventualities.

The investigator is further helped by the fact that not only does he share with all other men a point of affecting origin in the universal metaphor but also that he shares with all other men the concepts that, subsequent to the cultural metaphoric base, all men in all cultures divide their works into temporal, spatial, and temporal-spatial forms, that they all use the same media, and that all these media eventuate into the same forms, that is to say into sculpture, dance, etc.

One not only assumes that the work is amenable to study and that the investigator begins with certain advantages resident because he is human and a product both of his own and of human culture, but he also assumes that however much may vary the circumstances under which emotions are engendered and however much may vary the outward forms of their expression, nonetheless there is some universality of content in that all men love, hate, fear, exalt, feel anguish, despair, joy, and loneliness. It must be so, for beneath the fact that we are of different cultures lies the more basic truth that we are all men together. To assume

83

otherwise would be to assume the utter uniqueness of all men and render impossible the understanding not only of his affecting works, but also of his intellectual and social worlds as well. But we must admit nonetheless the intervention of the cultural variables. These include not only the influence of the cultural metaphoric base determining the fundamental relationship between feature and feeling, but factors of another sort which we might readily enough call epistemological. Thus at certain shrines among the Ibo, as reported by Robin Horton,[1] the most important carvings reside behind a screen and are never seen by the ordinary worshippers and seldom by the priests. The affecting import resides in the fact simply that the works are there—their presence alone, albeit unseen, is sufficiently important that an affecting situation is produced. Such epistemological variables may also prescribe that the affecting presence in effect exists only during certain ritual occasions; this is the case, for example, with many categories of masks which are kept in the rafters of their owners' houses at various locations in West Africa, to be brought forth only for important dances. Such a circumstance does not deny the affecting reality of the piece, however; it merely serves to point out that the affecting presence is, as affecting presence, operative only in rigorously defined situations rather than simply in repose. The concept of the affecting transaction is in such circumstances under the guise of performance rather than of gallery, and this fact does not accentuate the value of use over affect but merely prompts us to seek affect in use. It is very much as we in European cultures regard the opera or the ballet. Though they exist in one or another non-affecting condition at any time—in choreographic or musical notation— they do not come into affecting being as affecting presence until they exist in performance.

A further assumption is that every feature of each medium in every work is of potential aesthemic import. Subsequent to this, we assume that there are in the universe of feeling—as there are in the other areas of culture—patterns in operation preventing that disintegration into chaos which would render impossible institutions, words, and affecting works, with the exception that the latter two categories could occur on a purely idiosyncratic

[1] Robin Horton, *Kalabari Sculpture* (Apapa, Nigeria: Department of Antiquities, 1965).

16. *Bronze mask, Ife, Yoruba.*

basis, as they sometimes do among psychotics. The existence of patterning requires that we assume the presence of a system in the affecting world, and we have already taken this into account in acknowledging the existence of similetic metaphors, which we have defined as equivalence among those diverse forms which are commonly expressive of a common feeling. Finally we assume that the whole system is expressive of a basic grammar whose relatively limited terms include certain highly generalized assertions about the execution of media, the exercise of experience and relationality, the incorporation of intention, and the achievement of the affecting presence.

The affecting works of a culture can be studied by the same sequence of procedures used in the study of other phenomena: identification of the phenomena, observation and description, analysis, and ultimately generalization. Since the affecting presence is a particular kind of phenomenon, particular methods are required for each procedure, taking their point of departure in the nature of the materials.

It is not all cold system, however, for the affecting works are too various, subtle, and surprising. Even in a system like language or social structure, composed of units which are all of one physical sort (certain kinds of sounds constitute certain phonemes; certain kinds of social behavior betray certain kinds of social relationships), it is not always easy to sort and classify data. But there are in language and in social structure clear structural principles, and that one knows this is helpful in itself. One is certain that with adequate analysis of the data and scrupulous application of the principles, order should emerge. However, when the units of the system can be any type of physical data, from planes through sounds, the problem becomes more difficult. Further, we are not accustomed to thinking in terms of the fact that these works themselves are not random but fit into a system, albeit one of less discreteness, less fixity, less "tightness" than that of language or of social structure. The situation is further complicated by the fact that, unlike the other two systems where one kind of thing means one kind of thing and another means another, in the system of affecting works many really quite diverse data—diverse both within a medium and from medium to medium—can "mean" the same thing, in the sense that they are all addressed to a common affective state and are with respect to one another similetic. Further, a given work can simultaneously have multiple imports, because it is a configuration of affecting media and affecting properties and, indeed, of affecting intentions. Finally, among works showing what are apparently no more significant differences than among various utterances of the same word, there can be greater or lesser import.

To perceive order in a universe of forms and works so numerous requires a special sort of imagination. I should think a fairly steadfast one is indicated, one that does not permit beguiling differences to obscure basic identities which are present among the various works of a given culture and which indeed must be present, if momentarily hidden, for the simple reason that it is the nature of human behavior to be ordered. Imagination is essential to the perception of the affecting system and, ultimately, of the cultural metaphor. It is impossible to see how the operations leading to the factoring out of aesthemes can be conducted without the active play of a subtle, rich, free-ranging, and totally adventurous imagination, one that drives forward to the novel when the traditional does not prove relevant.

Identification of the Affecting Presence

It is not difficult to identify the classes of phenomena among which affecting works are to be found, for they are the traditional forms—sculpture, painting, dance, music, ritual, drama, narrative, poetry, and costume. It is obvious, however, that not all the members of these classes are affecting works—department store dummies, TV jingles, most billboard advertisements, the awarding of a Ph.D., the fox-trot—these are all clearly nothing more than parodies of serious works, if that much. They are not of the order of affecting presence, for affect is not presented by them and experience is not of their substance; they are without content. They are nothing but bits of business, mindless pleasures or annoyances. We must search for evidence of seriousness and mindfulness, value, feeling, import, content, and presentation if we are to identify the affecting presence.

Rite-relatedness

There are, nonetheless, a few behavioral points that frequently characterize the treatment accorded the affecting presence.

87

A work intentionally created to play a role in ritual, if it is a member of one of the forms enumerated in the first sentence of this discussion of identification, is almost invariably an affecting presence. One might quickly conclude that, given the criteria I have suggested, I am being over-cautious in stating that such objects and events are "almost invariably" affecting symbols. But this is not the case. Caution is warranted. I think of the life-size puppets which, carved without elegance, are clothed in official regalia and used in the second burial ceremonies for some of the chiefs among the Yoruba of Nigeria. It is the total impact which is of affective significance. As far as I am aware, no special treatment is subsequently given the puppet figure, and it cannot be presumed that the puppet itself was ever intended to be an affecting presence. On the other hand, the famous bronze and terra cotta heads of Ife, which some scholars maintain were used on such effigies, were subsequently taken to shrines where sacrifices were made to them and where they were generally regarded as being of great affective importance. Certainly in the case of the bronzes, these heads were made to endure long after the puppet body itself had been thrown aside and to be used as ritual objects in the shrines dedicated to the kings (oba).

This brings us to another kind of phenomenon related to the affecting presence and ritual, namely the fact that there are those works which are not simply used in ritual but are themselves the subjects of ritual. Indeed some of the heads mentioned above may possibly belong to this category. Certainly this is the case with the mud figures dedicated to the god Oduduwa at Igbodia, Ife, Nigeria.[2] In such cases there can be no doubt that what one is faced with is indeed an affecting presence. Further, it need not be only figures which are so regarded. There are other works which, as repositories of divine power, themselves receive ritualized attention. An example of such is the Golden Stool, which is the potent emblem of royal authority to the King (Asantehene) of the Ashanti people of Ghana. At the same time as the stool is an emblem of the kingship, it is also an affecting presence, the recipient of sacrifice, a most serious work executed with intention in the affecting media,

---

[2] For an example of this, see Frank Willett, *Ife and the History of West African Sculpture* (New York: McGraw-Hill Book Co., 1967), plate 108.

88

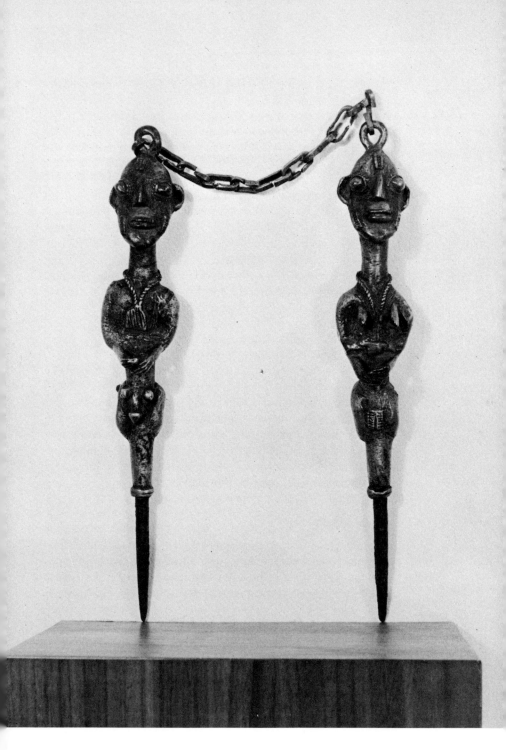

17. *Edan rods, Yoruba.*

and possessed of the affecting properties. It is, in essence, the portrait of a stool; and before one can appreciate the affect connected with the stool, he must recognize the importance of the stool as such throughout Ashanti. It is not, therefore, wholly unlike the bronze axes of the Oba of Benin or the jade adzes of Polynesia.

Affecting works are frequently of restricted audience as well. This may indeed have been the case with the Palaeolithic parietal art. Certainly it is true that the masks of the Yoruba Egungun dancers may not be seen by women or very young children. Women may not know the secrets of the bush school wherein young men are taught their part of the ritual life of the tribe, often through the use of the affecting presence. This is true of many peoples, in both middle Africa and in Oceania. Participation is restricted as well in those events where affect is involved: only men may attend the mosque; and in early Christianity, catechumens could not witness the most sacred mysteries of the mass.

The rite-relatedness of a work usually indicates that, for those perceptors who are co-cultural with the affecting presence in question, the transaction is a function of use. It is an open question whether the works have affecting significance when in repose. I suspect that in some instances they do, while in others they do not. In any event, this is a subject for ethnographic investigation which one hopes, having been called to mind, will in some instances at least be pursued.

Special Treatment

Simply because the affecting presence is a presence, it is cared for—loved, respected, feared, held in awe, judged in terms of goodness or badness, fed, and clothed. Thus affecting works tend to be given significantly different treatment from objects which are not valued in this particular way but which economically may be of equal or even greater worth. A Yoruba will treat a hoe much differently from the way he treats a twin figure, the former being kept in a secure place in the compound, to be sure, but the latter maintained in a shrine or carried about on the person of the mother of the actual twins. The Dogon of Mali bury their masks when they are not in use; and Palaeolithic man painted the walls of his caves with his superlatively executed

18. *Bronze group, Yemi Besiri, Yoruba.*

animals not at the caves' entrances, where they might have been of easy access and readily viewable in available light, but in the caves' far recesses, difficult to reach. We ourselves place in museums those works which we greatly honor as affecting works.

There are, of course, other factors to be considered. Each affecting presence is in specific ways (excellence, form, content, or context) unique and in terms of affecting-existence is of specific address, whereas any well-made hoe will do the job as well as any other. Affecting works are in part valuable because of their uniqueness. But there is the possibility that uniqueness becomes of affective significance itself. This is clearly the case in many countries of the world, for example in France or the United States. Further, affecting works are designed to present affect via the senses, and therefore they are delectable to the senses. Thus they are intended in most instances to be seen or heard, and special circumstances are often provided to assure optimal conditions for their being perceived by those who wish to do so.

In short, the affecting presence is characteristically treated in a way that is notably different from objects made at equal or even greater costs in labor and materials. Its treatment is more expensive than its objective cost would appear to lead one to anticipate. The affecting presence is housed in a special place (even in an individual home it is given special location; it is either secreted or given a place of focus and good light). It is honored—even in some cases venerated. Some are fed, even when the people hunger; and some are clothed in riches, in bewildering contrast to the poor attire of those who honor them.

I have spoken in terms of carvings, castings, masks, and—by implication—costumes. But the prerogatives of special treatment, of restricted audience, and of rite-relatedness are not reserved to sculpture alone. All the performed arts are subject to being executed in special places—sacred groves, temples, palaces, expensive concert halls and opera houses—and they frequently require special attire, on the part of both participants and audience. In some areas of the world, sacrifices must be made or ritual purification occur before the affecting presence may be enacted, as the fasting of the priest who intends to say the Mass, abstention from sexual intercourse by the Kalabari carver before he carves figures to the gods, ownership of songs and dances by Yoruba cult groups, rigorous definition of who among the dancers in various West African tribes may enjoy the consummate transactional experience of becoming possessed by the god, and so forth.

Not all objects and events which receive special treatment are affecting presences, however. There can be reasonable assurance that all objects and events so treated are probably involved with affect, but whether they are indeed affecting presences is quite another matter. A rock that hosts mana is not an affecting presence; neither is the act of menstruation among those peoples who exile menstruating women to special huts removed from the rest of the village. Nor are all objects and events which are rite-related affecting presences; witness the bell used to signal important moments in religious services and the umbrellas which cover the Asantehene of the Ashanti on ritual occasions. Drums used in many West African areas to sing the praise names of the gods, however, are specifically treated in such a way as to suggest that drums of this sort are affecting presences; such drums are carefully carved—sometimes with the attributes of human bodies—sacrificed to, and have names.

Observation and Description

What I have just discussed under "identification of the affecting presence" amounts to a kind of observation to be sure. But here I have something quite different in mind. *Study* might be an equally acceptable term. In either case, I mean to refer to that painstaking examination of the affecting works necessary in order for one to become intimately familiar with them, and intimate familiarity is the *sine qua non* of further operations.

I have already presented the frame of reference within which observation and description occur: a determination of the forms, an inventory of the affecting media used as well as of their properties, and a description of the affecting properties of the work. Specifically, the worker at this point gives careful examination and description also to the structure, style, surface, and substance of the work. The consideration of the work's content must be postponed until much later, when a greater knowledge and understanding characterize the worker's familiarity with the affecting universe.

93

Analysis

A corollary of the assumption that all features are candidates for affecting significance is that some of them *are* indubitably affecting—most of them, perhaps. We have already taken this into account in our earlier discussion of distinctive and accidental features. At any rate, it is the task of analysis to identify those features which are of affecting significance.

It is a further corollary of that same assumption that features which recur in any given form with such notable frequency that they may be said to be characteristic of works of the form may be assumed to be significant. We further assume that a significant characteristic has affecting significance in its own terms. In short, we are working at the level of aesthemics, earlier defined as those least common denominators of significant physical features in any given form.

In analysis, one is concerned with ascertaining the characteristic uses of the affecting media and their properties, particularly perhaps of relationality and the structure, style, and surface of the affecting properties of the whole. Presumably one will come to the point where it is possible also to identify meaningful configurations of features. Basic to this inquiry is a fundamental familiarity with the characteristics of affecting forms.

Granting knowledge and imagination about affecting forms, one may then make a series of examinations which are likely to reveal at least some of the meaningful configurations. Of all the forms, it is in sculpture and painting, and most especially in the representation of the human body, that one may commence his search. Further, one will choose the human body as it actually is as the standard against which to perceive deviations. It is apparent that one style of aesthetic configuration differs from another and that such differences can be perceived only in comparative terms. The choice of the natural human body as a model is arbitrary, but justifiable since its natural presentation is so well known that it therefore constitutes a reliable yardstick.

The chances are great that one will find deviations from the natural body, and so one must carefully note these in work after work, with the objective of cataloguing as complete as possible an inventory of such deviations. Differences will be of two sorts: variations from the body's form and variations from its features. Let us examine some works of the Yoruba.

94

We note, with respect to the form of the twin figure (fig. 4), that its head is large in comparison with its trunk, its legs are short and its arms long, and there is little sense of either elbow or knee. One is aware, however, of the presence of flesh over bones and of viscera within the abdomen. Further, the head is tilted. The features are greatly exaggerated. The sense organs are all too big for the face; the breasts are remarkable, in terms of both their size relative to the thorax and their conformation and suspension. There is no evidence of any attempt to render the fingers and toes in the round.

The next step is obvious. One attempts to discern among the deviations of form and feature the existence of patterns so that he may ascertain which deviations are meaningful and which are purely idiosyncratic. Accordingly we will examine three additional pieces—the carvings of a white man (fig. 6), a woman with twins (fig. 3), and another ibeji (fig. 5). Ordinarily this would hardly constitute a satisfactory universe, and indeed it does not here. It is an adequate sample of a universe, however, since analysis has demonstrated that were we to enlarge the sample one-hundredfold we would not significantly increase the range of patterned characteristics.

The three new specimens show us that the features noted in the first figure prevail here, with a few exceptions. The head is still very large, and even though two of the figures are not standing (one kneels, and the other sits), the size of the legs, while uniformly short, varies in shortness from one figure to the other; and the heads do not exhibit the same cocked quality. Knees and elbows are suggested or present in both the kneeling and seated figures. Some of these then are variables, while leg shortness, with respect to arms and trunk, and big-headedness are patterned constants.

Generalization

Analysis yields generalization, of course, in that it leads to an identification of aesthemes. All subsequent generalization, however, concerns aesthemic regularities both within and among the forms, i.e., the perception of the operation of the similetic metaphor among the forms, which amounts to para-aesthemics. Ultimately one is led to a description of the metaphoric system, culminating in the statement of at least some of the content of the cultural metaphoric base.

One must be aware of the characteristic of generalizations at these levels. In the first place, one must be ever aware that the frame of reference provided in this essay concerns nothing but the formal elements of the affecting presence—sculpture as sculpture, music as music, and so forth. Substance has no relevance except insofar as it constitutes imperatives for form. This is not to say that substance has no affecting significance; that would be absurd. Indeed, substance is that which is most readily available to the perceptor; it is substance that he knows he is perceiving. The formal problems with which we are here concerned are far subtler and in all probability lie beyond the levels of consciousness of the native perceptor. Further, since they are generalized and order vast numbers of instances of discrete works, these formal principles (aesthemes, para-aesthemes) have significance at the cultural level.

The characteristic of these further generalizations, then, is that they will resemble generalizations made about other areas of behavior at the cultural level. They will be offered as structurally true and will be understood to have been stated at the highest level possible, characterizing the principles of structure in at least a significant, if not a preponderant, body of instances.

The data upon which these generalizations with which we are now concerned are based are patterns factored out from those aesthemes one has identified by analysis. The scholar works wholly through each form to perceive the formal aesthemes, following the leads back through the objective metaphor and trope to the cultural metaphoric base. He also views the aesthemes cross-formally, or indeed cross-medially, in order to establish the identities which obtain irrespective of the physical differences among the forms and media. One works, indeed, to identify those patterns which, having their origins in the cultural metaphoric base, order works medially and formally as well as cross-medially and cross-formally into a single, affecting system. We assume that a patterned configuration of form or a patterned treatment of features is significant. The alternative is to assume that it is not significant and thus that there is no affective cause—nor indeed any reason of any sort—why the Yoruba carvers chose in so patterned a fashion

97

to deviate from the natural form of the human body. This alternative is entirely unacceptable, not because one assumes that every cultural thing or occurrence is fraught with subtle meaning, but because one is confident that there is a much better chance that a pattern is meaningful than that it is not.

Patterns in affecting presences, in this case sculptural ones, are meaningful as indicators of the cultural intention to convey particular kinds of formally presented affect. Insofar as these are viewed as particular in their involvement with a specific work, we are talking about the objective correlative, and insofar as they are viewed as general, we are talking of the formal metaphor, the objective metaphor, the trope, or the cultural metaphoric base.

The recognition of those cross-medial and cross-formal metaphoric equivalents we have called similes is the step in the method demanding the greatest amount of empathy and imagination. The techniques involved in perceiving the equivalents established by the process of simile require an extensive and responsive relationship with affecting works on the part of the investigator. He must have knowledge of the affecting potentialities of the various conditions of the medium's several physical properties and the variations of the relationships possible among those physical properties.

For example, in the European Romantic period, the somber in music; the sad in subject matter; the slowness and stateliness in movement and music; the long, flowing, and strong lines in sculptural or graphic forms—these all contribute toward producing a common affective re-creation in the perceptor. The experience and sensitivity which bring one to this perception of identity are instructive not only in that they show us something of the nature of cross-media identity in a particular respect but also in that they point to the impossibility—or at least the very great difficulty—encountered in trying to state in fairly explicit terms the "method" of making such discoveries.

The Criterion of the System

Aesthemes of the whole or of the part as revealed by analysis in the various media and forms must, granting the validity of our concept of a common affecting system, *mutatis mutandis,* have their counterparts in all the other media and forms. Any

98

20. Door, Yorub

feature or configuration of features, whether of structure or of style, which cannot be demonstrated to be the formal variant of an aestheme resident in the cultural metaphoric base—as evidenced by its similetic existence in other forms—is not a structural or stylistic aestheme. The only conceivable exceptions to this are those instances in which works of a given form may be imported (as in America we import works of Japanese sculpture) or copies (as African forms were copied or used as points of departure among Derain and his youthful colleagues). Barring either of these cases and given that the work or feature is not by the criterion of system an aestheme, one can conclude only that the feature in question is merely a common characteristic that may be pleasing but is not aesthemic.

A case in point would appear to be the feature of the exponential curve to which William Fagg and Margaret Plass direct our attention in *African Sculpture*. With a sure and sensitive eye for the pertinent, they point to the frequency with which the principle of the exponential curve occurs in West African sculpture. That the feature occurs only frequently rather than regularly and that it appears to occur randomly suggest, on the one hand, that it is not aesthemic on the whole and, on the other, that it is not aesthemic with respect to a given affect. This suspicion is heightened in that no evidence is offered for its similetic existence in other forms, nor does it seem to be characterizing other forms.

Needless to say the clear perception, based on the evidence, of what one believes to be an aestheme in one form may, after the exercise of diligent and disciplined imagination, prove indeed to be so. In the event that a characterization of the aesthemics of the affecting presences has already been essayed, and the contents of the cultural metaphoric base tentatively described, it is clear that re-description will have to be undertaken so that the new datum might be accommodated into the system.

The Affecting Presence
among the Yoruba

The nature of the affecting presence having been thus delineated, it is time now to turn to the affecting presence as it exists in a single culture, examining its characteristics at a high level of generalization and in various forms in order that we might perceive what uniformities we can. Since this is to be but a preliminary examination made for the purposes of illuminating the nature of metaphor and of demonstrating the wholeness of understanding its study will yield, I shall look solely for aes-themes at the level of affecting style and for para-aesthemes, so that we may establish an understanding of the system of simi-letic equivalents, perceiving at last the orders of the trope and the cultural metaphoric base. Further, I shall be concerned solely with formal metaphors.

I have chosen for this examination the affecting presence among the Yoruba, a numerous people, variously stated to be from 8 million to 10 million, who live in both villages and cities in the Western Region of Nigeria.[1] Traditionally, the Yoruba were governed by hereditary kings or oba supported by admin-istrative hierarchies of palace officials, chiefs, and elders. Now these officials govern in behalf of the federal government. Po-lygamy is practiced by the Yoruba. And since a man may have

[1] This study is concerned chiefly with late traditional forms, i.e., traditional forms as practiced in the villages during the last several decades. It does not in-clude recent, Europe-inspired innovations.

101

numerous wives, families are large, living in enclosed compounds. The family worships a pantheon of spirits—divine, heroic, and ancestral.

Sculpture

As is characteristic of most peoples of West Africa, the Yoruba have traditionally lived in the presence of a wealth of affecting works—sculpture, dance, music, ritual—and of myth; most but not all of these are dedicated to serious social and/or religious purposes. In some instances, the affecting works become instruments for the management of the supernatural. This is particularly evident in those instances in sculpture where the figure may be "fed" with sacrifices in order that the benefactions of the spirit-controlled powers might be won for the living. It is not alone in sculpture, however, that such instrumental ideals about the affecting presence prevail. In the maskings and dances of the Gelede society, it is the intention to so honor the idea of femininity that the pains of evil through witchcraft may not be visited upon the men.

Presumably, the Yoruba have a long tradition of affecting works. Since writing was not introduced into the culture until after contact with European civilization, however, there are no written documentations to this effect; and since their works in wood would have been destroyed by the climate or by insects, all that remains for us to use as evidence are works in metal or in terra cotta. Fortunately these works are relatively numerous, and the assiduous and intelligent labors of such archaeologists as Bernard Fagg and Frank Willett have reconstructed the major outlines of a history for us.

The area north of the confluence of the Niger and Benue rivers is presumed to be the site of an ancient civilization, perhaps even one much older than the Nok culture, which can be identified as having thrived there fully developed and with a marked degree of technological achievement from at least the middle of the first millennium B.C. until several centuries after the beginning of the Christian era. We know this culture chiefly through the terra cotta fragments which have been recovered, and both William Fagg and Frank Willett point to stylistic and architectonic factors which argue the continuity of the tradition from Nok through the present day.² The wood-carving tradition is older than even the terra cotta heads from Nok, as is evidenced by the presence in the terra cottas of schema to suggest the presence of a wood-carving tradition.

The Nok heads (figs. 10, 11) do not share features with only Yoruba affecting works, however. The Nomoli (fig. 12) of Sierra Leone and the Krinjabo heads (fig. 13) of the Akan peoples of the Ivory Coast both appear to share stylistic affinities with the traditions of Nok. There is a suggestion that Nok (or some culture antecedent to it) was the paleotype of the cultures of West Africa, at least insofar as their sculptural productions are concerned.

The great bronzes of Ife, dating from about the fourteenth century (figs. 14, 15, 16), are certainly Yoruba works, and we presume that their naturalism, which Willett sees as bearing traces of style that place them within the continuity of tradition from Nok, was wholly inspired by indigenous canons concerning the realization of the affecting presence. We must also take into consideration that there existed simultaneously a viable tradition of wood carving, a tradition which derived directly from the schema of the Nok period and which was transitional from those forms to the recent, traditional wooden forms—the ibeji (figs. 4, 5), for example. These works would have contrasted markedly with their contemporary, royal, Ife portrait heads.

The period around the fourteenth century at Ife, then, was characterized by a vigorous and strikingly diversified activity in the production of affecting works of sculpture—works which beneath the difference in their two chief fashions yet bore to one another the deep relationships of common familiality. One is tempted to assert, though the lack of evidence denies him legitimate opportunity, that such diversity might also have characterized the other affecting forms during that same period. Thus dance and music might also have exhibited such diversities similarly clustering about the two social poles of the royalty and the proletariat.

The recent traditional period of sculpture, dating from the beginning of European colonization, is also rich—in production,

² William B. Fagg, *Tribes and Forms in African Art* (New York: Tudor Publishing Company, 1965), and Frank Willett, *Ife and the History of West African Sculpture* (New York: McGraw-Hill Book Co., 1967), pp. 183–201.

if not in the great variety of materials and styles which characterized the fourteenth century. The process of casting in bronze
by the lost-wax method continued (figs. 18, 19), as demonstrated
in the pieces from the secret Ogboni society. The spatial works
are numerous in quantity and diverse in kind, as may be seen
by comparing these bronzes with the other recent traditional
pieces (figs. 19–23). In these works, the human form is the most
common subject matter. The human body may be represented
in the round or in relief; the former pieces are found in shrines,
memorials, and utilitarian works such as those supporting bowls
(fig. 19) and roofs, and the latter on doors (fig. 20).

With the exception of the bronze works of Ife, portraiture—
at least in the highly individualized sense familiar to the European—has not characterized Yoruba sculpture. There are the
ibeji, carved in honor of twins, but although these figures cor-
respond by sex to the twin "represented," whether they are to
represent particular twins or twins in general is by no means
clear at this point. This absence of individualization by portraiture is hardly surprising, given that most sculptures have
been of generic types (e.g., Ifa and Shango priestesses, ibeji).

Other forms (fig. 23 and frontispiece) are executed in the round
as well—notably the chicken, which has ritualistic significance
as a sacrificial victim and which as a mythological figure
scratched sand upon the primordial waters, thus creating land.
The Yoruba also create a variety of masks, ranging from the
simple (fig. 24) to the complex (figs. 25, 26). All these masks exhibit the characteristic feature of displaying the facial features
pulled together, seeking centrality in a context which is otherwise too big for them. Finally, the recent traditional period of
Yoruba works appears to be versatile in subject matter, as is
evidenced in the district officer in his boat, carved shortly after
the turn of the twentieth century by Thomas Ona (fig. 6).

It is the figures in the round in wood which will concern us
here. These figures are more typically associated with religious
activities. Equally typically, the Yoruba figure stands, although
kneeling and sitting figures are also relatively common. These
latter figures often tend to give the illusion of greater height than
standing figures. Compare the ibeji with the Ilesha figure (fig. 3);
the head of the kneeling figure is as great in total volume as
that of the standing figure. Thus, while the two classes of figures
are of similar height, one stresses the execution of the full,

104

upright body, and the other, the representation of the kneeling body from the knees up. In the Ilesha figure in particular, the illusion of greater height is increased by the arm length, which is much greater than that of the ibeji.

As we have seen, the Yoruba also depict the human figure in the role of supporting house or utensil, or indeed another figure, and carve it in relief on doors (fig. 20). They work in metal as well, as is evidenced by the edan figures and the group from the Ogboni society (fig. 18). Although this latter work is superficially quite dissimilar from the other pieces in terms of the rich and complex treatment given the headdress, nonetheless beyond such idioms one may see the traditional Yoruba point of departure with respect to the interpretation and treatment of the features of the face—the bulbous, applied eyes, nose, mouth, and ears, and their centripetal interrelationships.

In general, the head of the human figure in sculpture is somewhat idealized, with an expression that those familiar with the sculpture of the Yoruba recognize as typical composure; the features appear to be applied to the surface of the face. Whether in the round or in relief, the head-to-trunk relationship of the body is seldom in accordance with the head-to-trunk relationship of the human body; the head is generally oversized. Further, the trunk-to-legs relationship is also at variance with that of the human form, with the legs in general being smaller than they should be were they to conform to naturalistic proportions. Indeed, the head-trunk-legs ratio, more often than not, appears to be more nearly that of a baby than of an adult, and when this proportion of infancy is combined with the typically adult face and genitalia, characteristic tension results. Probably a less dramatic range of proportional variation from the adult human form is exhibited among the cast metal figures or among those done in relief than among those carved in the round. The former bear a *closer* relationship to the actual human form, but a pattern of structural variation is still present and in similar terms.

In the presentation of the human figure, there is a distinct preference for the vertical lines of the body, with primary emphasis being given to the long column of the body from the top of the head through the trunk to the feet. Indeed, the hyperbolic structural statement of the head tends to de-emphasize its roundness

106

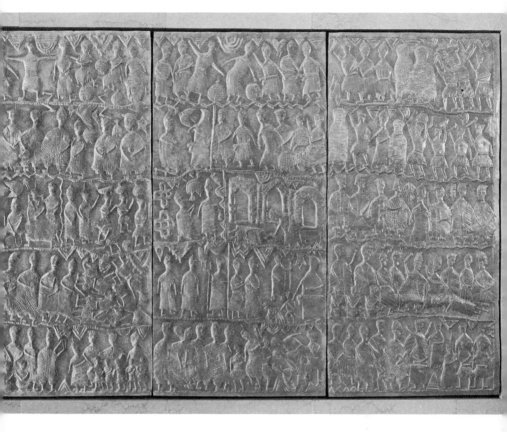

22. *Aluminum panel in relief, Asiru Olatunde, Yoruba.*

by giving it a structural weight almost akin to that of the trunk, often accentuating the long lines of the face. It is as though there were a clear aesthetic imperative which operates to reduce the body to a continuous vertical volume. And the same imperative seems to require that the head of the piece bear a constant proportion to the actual height of the piece rather than to its implied height so that, as we have seen, the head of a kneeling figure requires the same volume in proportion to actual height that the head of a standing figure does.

The inference is that the sculptural works of the Yoruba *present* by means of an unconscious and culturally patterned style that is characterized by intensive continuity. I shall proceed to write analytically of certain works which are stylistically representative of the universe of Yoruba works.

There are in sculpture only a limited number of ways in which intensionality can, in gross terms, exist: laterally, frontally, or totally. The Ibibio doll (fig. 7) exhibits lateral intension; the Akua-ba figure of the Ashanti, with its vestigial arms extending minimally into lateral space and with all ventral and dorsal features dramatically understated if not, indeed, non-existent, shows frontal intension (fig. 27); finally, the ivory figure from the Lega people exhibits total intension, such that the piece is scarcely far removed from the naturally rounded shape of the ivory from which it was carved (fig. 28).

The works of the Yoruba exhibit a fourth possibility: they are characterized by both lateral and frontal intension. This is a condition which must be distinguished from total intension and may be seen by noting in the Yoruba works the absence of the roundness of the Lega figure as well as the absence of its minimal definition and separation of limbs from, and of facial and anatomical features upon, the core of the body.

The stylistic discipline of intension exists in each of the constitutive media of sculpture. In considering the medium of volume, there are different ways to describe it; but in terms of our discussion here, to describe volume in terms of its stylistic disciplines is to describe it in terms of its affecting characteristics—those which, considerable examination has revealed, are stylistically essential for the work to be Yoruba and not accidental or idiosyncratic.[3] Thus, of those volumes which constitute

[3] This is not to say that such features cannot be affecting, only that they are not *culturally* so.

108

23. *Ifa divination bowl, Yoruba*

the limbs, we say that the legs are characteristically short while the arms are characteristically long. But length is not really a feature of intension, since intension and extension refer to the placement in space with respect to a vertical line from head to feet. In these terms, then, we observe that the ibeji, for example, are carved with their arms slightly bowed, but nonetheless stiff at the sides of the body, and with the legs straight. The absence of any bending emphasizes their lack of frontal extension, as does the general absence of any sharply defined knee structure. There is a pervasive tendency to construe the legs as continuous volumes, not strikingly differentiated into upper and lower leg.

With respect to intension, the arms and legs are not as intensive as are the sculptures of the Baoule (fig. 29) or the Lega (fig. 28); neither are they as extensive as those to be seen in the Temne female figure (fig. 30), which in its totality more greatly exploits extensionality than do the Yoruba figures. An exception to this is the Yoruba reclining female (fig. 34), a piece which is unusual not in terms of the fact that it reclines, nor even in terms of its necessary curvatures in space (since reclining requires various extensive accommodations of the body), but in terms of the richness and complexity of its exploitation of extensional space.

Paradoxically, arms may extend into space without being extensional. In the case of the Ifa bowl (fig. 35), four female figures surmount the lid, their arms extended toward one another, each placing her hands upon the shoulders of the women on either side. The result is enclosure, a condition of intensionality.

In some instances, volumes will extend into space precisely because the anatomical features being depicted so extend. Examples of this are to be found in the trunk of the small silver elephant (fig. 36) and in the ram's head (fig. 37). The extent to which a horn or a hornlike ornament *may* extensionally exploit space can be seen in the Bambara chi-wara (fig. 38) and in the Ekoi head (fig. 39).

The head and neck must be considered in terms related to these; and with the head inevitably intruding upward into space, the question is how intensionality or extensionality characterizes the sculptured heads of the Yoruba. The heads of figures in wood, bronze, or ivory are invariably characterized by very large eyes, large nose and mouth, and large ears. The facial

110

24. *Gelede mask, Yoruba.*

features, indeed, command more of their share of the face's surface than is the natural case. The head terminates usually in a pointed coiffure or hat and is set upon a columnar neck. Certainly the necks of the figures of the Ifa bowl (fig. 35) represent the extreme of this latter tendency. These forms extending into space are, however, modest in their spatial demands, in their rhetoric, as it were. There is no evidence of the exploitation of extension for its own sake. Once again, contrast the Yoruba and the Ekoi heads, as noted above. Or examine the Benin heads, where elaborate attention to the finials of crown, beard, collars, and jewels attests the delight taken in the elaborate exploitation of space (figs. 40, 41, 42).

Of facial features, one can speculate that extensionality would be characterized by a pushing of the features to the periphery of the face, at the expense of their natural interrelationships, and the result would be surrealistic. On the other hand, there can be little doubt that the facial features of the Akua-ba of the Ashanti (fig. 27), all drawn together into one small area of the face, clearly suggest intensionality. Although the Yoruba facial features on their sculptures are large, occupying nearly all the facial area, the normal relationships among them have not been violated by means of the influence of any dispersive centrifugality. On the other hand, they are clearly not as *intensional* with respect to their context as are the facial features of the Akua-ba.

It is interesting to note, in passing, the fashion in which a Yoruba carver exploits frontal intensionality in carving the head of a horse (fig. 25). Whether he works in wood or in ivory, the artist restricts frontal extension, executing the head as nearly as possible in a vertical plane parallel with the body of the rider. The normal set of the horse's head upon his neck is disregarded, as consequently is the fact that in its normal position, the head tends to be more nearly parallel with the earth than vertical to it.

There is not a similar inhibition upon the frontal extension, however, in the treatment of the features of the thorax and the abdomen. Breasts, genitalia, and buttocks often tend to thrust exaggeratedly into space (see the ibeji figures). But otherwise the body shows unmistakable evidences of the stylistic discipline of intension and is in general executed with minimal modeling, in contrast, for example, with the Lega (fig. 28), who show markedly less modeling.

112

25. *Epa mask, Yorub.*

I assume that a drive toward the presentation of extensionality may exploit modeling as a means of exploiting space, whereas the presentation of intensionality will foster the opposite tendency. I am, of course, speaking of the overwhelming tendency of Yoruba wood carving in this respect, but by no means am I including *all* of it. Refer, for example, to the ibeji (fig. 44) with the major muscular areas of his body shown in exaggerated and dramatic modeling.

It is not only in terms of the unimportance of modeling, however, that one is to discern evidence of intensionality. The Yoruba sculptures in the round eloquently bespeak an interest in the presentation of verticality that would otherwise be destroyed by bending the body at the waist or at the knees. Even the offertory piece (fig. 3), which is theoretically bent by virtue of her kneeling position, has the extensional effects of kneeling minimized by radically understating the size and protrusion of her bent legs and by having the feet retroflexed in upon themselves so that they also avoid extending too far beyond the body's intensional, vertical midline. Naturally, by the laws of nature, the seated human body, or the body on horseback, cannot as readily show its legs as subordinated to the verticality of the body. They must extend at right angles from the trunk of the body.

Masks significantly present three distinct facial types. There is first that type often to be encountered in the Egungun mask (fig. 45), which often appears to be a greatly enlarged version of the same face we see upon the ibeji. Another is the Epa mask (figs. 25, 26), a complex sculptured entity whose face tends to be less human, more anonymous, more geometrically abstracted than the other masks; it is, however, like the Egungun mask, also clearly representational of a human being in respect to the distribution of features. The faces of the Egungun and the Epa masks conform to all that was earlier said of the faces of the figures: the features tend to fill all or most of the available facial area. The face of the Gelede mask (fig. 24)—the third facial type—on the other hand, exhibits a strong trace of centripetality, suggestive of the face of the totally unrelated Akua-ba (fig. 27) of the Ashanti. The fact that much of this "gathering" of the facial features into a relatively small area of the face is due to foreshortening, necessary because the mask is worn on top of the head and the face is thus perceived by looking up at it, does not wholly explain

114

26. Epa mask, Bamgboye of Odo-Owa, Yoruba

this centripetality; the features could as easily be dispersed over a wider area of the available facial area.

Relief carving in general shows figures conforming, *for the most part,* to the features here set forth. There is, however, somewhat of a tendency to show them in extension, though by no means in maximal extension, as when they are viewed in contrast with the Javanese figures (figs. 8, 9). That this relative extension of the Yoruba reliefs is *in relief* is not sufficient to explain this difference between the figures in relief and those in the round, for figures in the round can readily be carved in maximal intension. What more nearly accounts for the differences between the two cases, I think, is the narrative quality often found in these relief carvings. The narrative milieu demands gestures, transportation, and other physical indications of action.

The second affecting medium of sculpture to be considered is *surface,* which has as its properties area, plane, roundness, angularity, and finish. As *surface* in sculpture is a function of volume, however, little more can be said of it than was said of volume. That is, in those cases where volumes are intensive, so also are the surfaces intensive. But the property of finish is a wholly different concern, for finish is a property of surface which, with respect to volumes, is an independent variable.

Not only is the finish of the surface of Yoruba sculptures characteristically smooth, but some of the research of Robert F. Thompson [4] attests that the Yoruba specifically judge smoothness of finish as being a prized characteristic of a piece. The surfaces of Yoruba works are sometimes paid homage with palm oil, or with cam wood, kaolin, or indigo. If the smoothness of the Yoruba works is not *clearly* indicative of a positive evaluation placed upon intensionality, it is in relative terms more nearly intensional than is the bumpy encrustation of the surface sometimes encountered among the works of other peoples. Further evidence of the appreciation of smoothness is to be found in certain ibeji and Shango pieces where the facial features have been worn down from the frequent attentions given them (washing them, rubbing them, or otherwise caring for the smoothness of their finish). It is usually the case with a Yoruba work of other than the softest wood that the finish is characterized by a deep, subtle, and thoroughly satisfying glow—like that of healthy skin.

[4] Robert F. Thompson, "Esthetics in Traditional Africa," *Art News* 66 (1968): 66.

116

27. *Akua-ba, Kumasi, Ashan*

But the Yoruba is not interested solely in smoothness of surface. At the same time, he inevitably shows the characteristic three scars on each cheek and sometimes even very elaborate patterns of scarification, as is to be seen on the back, arms, and chest of the kneeling woman (fig. 3). It is worth noticing in passing that, in contrast with the cicatrization of the Baoule figures, these are intaglioed rather than cameoed.

Situationality, the third medium, is the work's substantive factor. This substantive element, if it is to be properly identified, is usually to be encountered at the most particular rather than at the most general level possible. A portrait thus is "a portrait of x" rather than a portrait in general, and the situational medium is individuated and made to constitute a discrete work.

In Yoruba wood carving, however, the particular is seen in terms of its class membership. Although there are individuating features of each work so that one may be distinguished from another and either more or less highly prized, an ibeji, though carved in connection with a particular twin, is in situational terms *about* the reason for which ibeji are carved. It is generally the case that among the Yoruba, situational individuation does not characterize the works. Thus one adds to the first injunction —that of *seeking the encounter with the situationality of the work*—the further injunction that the encounter must be sought *at the most particular level possible.*

Yoruba intensional situationality involves minimal about-ness; extensional situationality is the opposite end of the continuum. Contrasting an ibeji with the Laocoon provides an example of each type. There appears now and again to be complexity of situationality among the works of the Yoruba—the Ogboni bronze (fig. 18) is an example of this, as is the Epa mask whose crown is composed of numerous individual figures (fig. 26). The reliefs carved upon doors (fig. 20) also seem to be of this type. But in one major respect, the earlier examples have a dominant characteristic which distinguishes them from the relief carving: they do not *as works* involve an about-ness; they are, rather, assemblages of individual situations. It is a further characteristic of intensional situationality that its about-ness is of a static estate, whereas that of the extensive work is of a kinetic one. Not only do we see this in the contrast between the ibeji and the Laocoon, but also in a contrast of ibeji with a dancing Siva, with its multiple pairs of arms. The rigorous patterning of the mode of figure

118

execution into the most economical of vertical structures, with a uniform drive toward intensionality expressed in ways that also are highly patterned, suggests a highly restricted inventory of meaningful kinds of relationships among the constituent parts of works.

At this initial point, one can perceive only the most readily presented categories of relationships, for now we do not even perceive that universe of special "logic" which pervades the affecting world and its works, which governs each work, which governs each form, and which, *mutatis mutandis,* governs all the forms. We do not even perceive now all the possibilities of *kinds* of relationships which may obtain. In addition to spatial and temporal relationships of before and after, contiguity, continuity, greater and less, faster and slower, are there relationships also of entailment, for example? Is there a special category of "truth" and "falsity" which is superordinate to affecting relationships? Are there categories and conditions of relationships we have not even suspected? And finally, under all the circumstances listed above, what are the characteristics, in these terms, of intensionality and extensionality, continuity and discontinuity?

At this point, I can say nothing except what must appear most obvious: intensional relationality, whatever its complexities and its subtleties, is characterized by closure and by enclosure. *Closure* designates the relationships among constitutive volumes, surfaces, and situations—and those interpenetrating and internecessitating relationships among all the facets, uses, and features of all these media and their properties. These relationships are such that intervening spaces among volumes, complexities and radical contrasts of planar and textural properties of surface, and bifurcatory and ramifying extravagances of range of situation —all of these are in general inhibited rather than maximized. In addition, the angles of relationship between any two volumes are such that they are either significantly more or significantly less than 90°. *Enclosure* designates the total product of all instances of closure, such that the whole effect of a work is intensive rather than extensive—as may be seen, for example, in any of the ibeji, where as a function of the severely reduced angles between thorax and arm at the armpit, and between wrist and hip, the arms appear as enclosers of the body.

As the experience of space appears to be most significant for the Yoruba when it is intensive, so the experience of the second order of space, second-order temporality, is most pregnant with feeling when it is continuous. The existence of continuity in a work is a function of many of the factors which also produce intensionality—for example, the characteristic of low modeling, the desire for smoothness, the inhibition of the complexity and the radical contrasts of planes and textures, the reduction of the occurrence of right angles, and the drive toward closure. On the other hand, continuity is not solely a function of these conditions, as may be seen in some of the contemporary Makonde work which in its totality is yet characterized by intensive continuity (fig. 43).

One may distinguish two kinds of continuity, that achieved by using flowing volumes, surfaces, situations, and relationships, and—less obviously—that derived from an atomistic approach to the constitution of the affecting presence. A Baoule ancestor figure exemplifies the first approach and the paintings of the Pointillists, the second. One might think that with respect to sculpture, the simple requirements of two- or three-dimensional existence would prohibit a work's being executed either in discontinuity or in the atomistic approach to continuity. But such is clearly not the case. Discontinuity comes to exist in a work not because parts are discrete and physically unrelated (though this can be the case in constructivist works), but because points of juncture are exploited for the purposes of affecting significance, with the result that the work occupies not only as much space as possible (the dancing Siva), but also with as great a degree as possible of interruption of volumes and surfaces. The Wayang puppet (figs. 8, 9) shows something of this phenomenon. Atomistic continuity can be found in assemblages when the constitutive units, showing continuity themselves, also contribute to the intent toward continuity evident in the whole work. The prime example of this is the Epa mask (fig. 26), where the top is composed of a complex of continuous figures striving toward the solidity and continuity of the original tree trunk. Another example is the carved ivory horse, horseman, and woman, which have the details of their execution subordinated to the act of maintaining the continuous volume of the tusk, which yet manages to endure (fig. 21).

The instances of continuity in the Yoruba pieces are more apparent than those of intensionality. Accordingly, little needs to be said of it. The de-emphasis of the body's joints which one generally observes in Yoruba works, the understating of arm bends as in the woman with twins (fig. 3), and the quality of low modeling serve to enhance the work's continuity. The preempting of nearly all available space by the sense features in the faces of figures can be viewed as an expression of continuity—as a continuum constituted of the sense organs—quite as readily as can the overstating of the empty surfaces of the face which characterize the Gelede mask (fig. 24). Certainly one will see the emphasis placed upon the trunk of the body, at the expense of the legs, as deriving from the obvious columnarity of the trunk and its natural affinity toward the expression of continuity. The overstatement and oversimplification of long volumes, deriving from the violation of their actual proportions and from the minimization of their modeling, lead simultaneously to a simplification of surfaces and relationships, the latter by means of quantitative reduction. Because situationality in sculpture in general is simple and instantaneous, the concept of continuity is here irrelevant. All the foregoing refers only to the carving of figures in the round. In relief carving, the case is somewhat different, with a greater use of body juncture in evidence, even though in many such carvings there tends to be a rounding off of the joints.

The history of the Yoruba also provides evidence of these points, although it is rare, since complete figures are most difficult to come across and are spread over more than two thousand years of history, the greatest portion of which is undocumented by written records. A few pieces which lend support to our argument come from the Nok culture, which thrived in the area north of the confluence of the Niger and Benue rivers, from at least 300 B.C. It may be considerably older, since this date is that attributed to the sophisticated formal style in which those terra cotta heads and figures which have been recovered were executed. Equally, it is surmised that the Nok culture continued beyond that period, perhaps merging in the ensuing centuries into that culture which produced the great bronze works of Ife as well as the continuing tradition of Yoruba wood carving. One

122

sees in the Nok face (figs. 10, 11) some of the same characteristics he sees in the recent Yoruba works, such as a similarly
conventionalized fashion of representing facial features and dis-
tributing them on the face.[5]

Of even more dramatic and conclusive note are the fragment
of legs (fig. 46) and the monkey (fig. 47). Even though curved,
the legs yet exhibit a clear interest in continuity, quite as markedly
as does the very differently conceived trunk of the monkey's
body. Note the understatement given the knee as a point of
articulation and the low modeling—to such an extent indeed
that any sense of muscular conformation is quite lost. The ankle,
in effect, does not exist at all; the leg is disarticulately inserted
directly into the foot, much as is the convention among recent
Yoruba wood-carvers. Though the legs display a great interest
in curves, they nonetheless at the same time have been placed
close together, in a frontal plane, thus demonstrating a concern
for intensionality. The bronze figure from Tada (fig. 48), dating
from somewhere between "early fifteenth century . . . and the end
of the sixteenth century," is, according to Willett—in a judgment
whose justification one must readily accept—perhaps the most
remarkable of the Ife works.[6] Like the Nok fragment, it too is
tortuously intensive.

The sculptural tradition of the Yoruba in general asserts intensive
continuity. At the same time, however, it is readily apparent that
these works are not as markedly intensive and continuous as the
works of the Baoule or the Lega. There exists a continuum from
intensive to extensive and from continuous to discontinuous;
it is not a case of either/or. In the seated bronze from Tada, in
the Ife heads, and even—by contrast with the Lega figure—in
the ibeji, there is an overriding drive toward naturalism, a drive
which must in some respects mitigate or condition the dedication
to intensive continuity.

Intensive continuity represents only two of the parameters of
the spatial existence of sculpture, albeit two critical ones. Intensive continuity does not totally account for the Yoruba sculpture—it does not fully explain the conventionalized proportions

[5] Frank Willett, Ife and the History of West African Sculpture (New York:
McGraw-Hill Book Co., 1967), pp. 183–201.
[6] Ibid., p. 168.

124

of the body, for instance. There is little doubt, however, that the principles behind these phenomena, after searching and imaginative thought, will prove amenable to careful and sensible formulation.

I have commented upon all the affecting media except *experience*. This is the inward medium, that flash of relevance and quality which the artist is able to create as a special physical condition in his work. It is a medium which builds from all the others, and all one can say is that within the area circumscribed by naturalism and by intensive continuity, the Yoruba artist finds—and appears to have found for at least over two millennia —those conditions where the affecting presence can exist meaningfully as a presentation of affecting consciousness.

Dance and Music

We have completed relatively full analyses of forms which are spatial. In the next chapter we shall consider narrative, which is temporal. Although each of these forms exists *primarily* in either space or time, each has an added dimension in which its complement can be construed in effect to exist. One may say of these inferred, complementary dimensions that they exist *in effect*, because the dimension of temporality in sculpture, or of spatiality in narrative, is not in fact really present but invented through what amounts to a second-order metaphorical process. Sculpture thus is essentially spatial, but via spatial means temporality is achieved; narrative is essentially temporal, but by means of synchronic complexity the functional equivalent of space is achieved. So it is in music. By means of materials which exist preeminently in time, there exists a second-order phenomenon which gives breadth and spread by means of special exploitation of temporal phenomena.

These primary and secondary space-time spindles of being, subject among the Yoruba to the disciplines of intensive continuity, are to be seen as well in both dance and music. Although I am not a proficient analyst in these two forms, since I have been trained in neither of them, and although my experience with both is markedly more limited than my experience with and my ability to analyze sculpture and narrative, nonetheless what I have experienced reveals to me that dance and music too exhibit the

126

31. *Monolith, Ife, Yoruba*

influences of the shapings of intensive continuity. This is, of course, what one would expect if he accepts the premise that all the affecting forms of a people reveal common features and are thus related one to the other as members of a system. His expectations in this respect are even more reasonable if he further expects that the more homogeneous a culture—by which I mean the less it has been ameliorated or distorted by acculturative impacts—the more one may expect tightness of structure, if not economy of terms, in the affecting system. One knows, therefore, that equivalences exist; he must only identify them. This the perceptive person can do even if his analytical concepts are not as powerful here as they are in sculpture and in narrative.

Dance.   For dance of course, as for music, there are no records to help us, for no systems of notation had been developed which would have preserved at least something of them. There cannot thus be any question of historical depth to our considerations of these forms.

Not only can there be no historical depth to such study, but the archival materials, especially on the dance, are rare indeed. In addition, there are few analyses, even for what materials do exist, in terms which would be useful to us here. The notations with which recent scholars have recorded dances and musical performances are, while adequate for the purposes for which they were employed, descriptive of simple physical execution and are not addressed to the affecting considerations to which our attentions here must be directed.

The body in the synchronic dimensions of the dance is presented in a fashion that asserts the same values as sculpture. This generalization, however, must be modified in terms of two factors: in all cases, since dance is movement, extremities will be used for locomotion and balance; and further, since dance is a presentation of action or interaction, the extremities will be used for their normal expressive purposes. This is particularly true where a stylized naturalism characterizes the affecting works. It is by extremes that one may define those dances in which extension is exploited far more than or far less than these "normal" requirements for balance and gesture. Certainly the dance of Java or of Bali establishes a clear point at which extensionality is richly and purposively exploited for its own sake. The dances one sees from Guinea Coast Africa, on the other

128

hand, where extension is rigorously avoided, define the other extreme.

Among the Yoruba, the head, shoulders, trunk, and legs are treated as a continuous system of long volumes, and as such they receive the dominant balletic attention. In general, dance is a matter of thrust—head, trunk, shoulder—with minimal interest in the hands and feet as instruments of affecting presentation, except insofar as they make contributions to the total rhythmic presentation of the dance. The feet, flat against the surface of the earth, shuffling and stomping, receive none of the careful expressive attention given to the feet in the European or the Javanese ballet; and in no instance that has come to my attention may one encounter a long, graceful, attenuated arc, carefully drawn with the arm, from the shoulder to the fingertips. The core of the body is a single instrument to which the extremities appear to be, if not irrelevant, at least lacking that great dramatic import attached to them in other traditions of the dance. It is the features of the core to which expression is relegated—the eyes, the mouth, the head itself, the shoulders, the breasts, the stomach, the buttocks—at every instant one or another of these areas or organs is bound to execute its own movements. Sometimes indeed more than one—perhaps all—will be the center of expressive activity simultaneously.

As in sculpture, then, the head-trunk-legs continuum of the body is chiefly emphasized at the expense of the extremities. Also as in sculpture, facial features, breasts, and buttocks achieve particular attention. In the dance as in sculpture, the affecting result of this focus upon the parts of the core is to give more dramatic assertion to the core itself rather than merely to focus the attention upon the various parts which are subject to movement. In other words, the assertion of the core of the body is made possible by means of the constituent assertions of its component parts.

The volumes asserted in dance then are truncal, and the relationships of the constituent areas and parts are in relation to those truncal volumes, as parts are to the whole. Movement is thrusting and rapid rather than gracefully attenuated and leisurely.

Miss Peggy Harper, Senior Research Fellow in Dance at the University of Ife in Nigeria, has, in personal correspondence, been understandably reluctant to generalize to the degree I

129

have done here; she has kept in mind the myriad exceptions and ambiguities.

In a checklist of dance studies, however, she permits herself to deliver a generalization which I cite, adducing it as general evidence in support of my view.

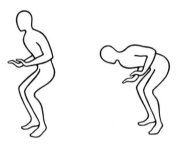

The positions in these diagrams (the back straight, the head and neck continuing the line of the back, the knees relaxed and slightly bent, legs and feet parallel with the feet firmly placed on the earth) are typical of many forms of dance in Africa. The back may be upright or incline at a slight or accute pelvic angle towards the ground surface. *The overall body position and accompanying movement give a kinetic sensation of moving into the earth or of a close and confident relation to the earth.* This in sharp contrast to many styles of European dance where the spatial accent is on an upright body which continuously tries to escape the force of gravity and the ground surface on which the dance is performed.[7] (The italics are mine.)

So much, then, for the Yoruba dance in its synchronic existence.

One often has the notion in some Yoruba dance, as in Samoan dance, that the body in dance is less a body in balletic movement than it is another musical instrument; and because it is a moving musical instrument it executes its own rhythmic function, in both movement and sound, becoming part of the musical totality. As such it is an agent of time and not of space, embodying an interest in the flux of repeated movement, sustaining by means of continued repetition what it cannot otherwise sustain. In its atomistic beats of truncality, becoming intricately part of the music itself, the body of the Yoruba in dance contrasts with that of the European dancer, whose carefully formulated positions may be sustained or may be quick, but flawlessly evolve from one into the other. Indeed, this is the case also

[7] Peggy Harper, "Dance Studies," *African Notes,* vol. 4 (Ibadan, Nigeria: Institute of African Studies, University of Ibadan, 1968), p. 22.

130

32. Mask, Bamilek

with the dancer from Java in his succession of distal extensions elaborately created in space, showing a very slight degree of the genetic relationships among successive positions. It would be interesting as well as revealing, I think, to treat the trunk and its expressive areas as separate rhythmic functions, plotting their activities with respect to the voices of the various drums which accompany the dance.

Music. The temporal equivalent of those long, lightly modeled volumes that assert continuity—the second-order spatiality of music—we must view as time-as-filled-as-possible-with-discrete-sound-happenings. Actually, a machine gun being fired enjoys this characteristic, and so does rain; but such events lack meaningful sound interest. So in order to make time as dense as possible with sounds and yet avoid monotony and chaos, varying voices and rhythms are used. Thus, although the simple, ongoing unity of time is asserted, that assertion is made with careful form, for it is imposition of form where chaos would otherwise reign which makes possible the creation of the affecting presence.

Musical time among the Yoruba seems most frequently to be so densely filled with rapid, interlocking beats that the music is less an analysis of time—though an analysis it is—than the presentation of time itself. The sounds are as dense as matter, and to the unaided ear the individual atoms of sound are too fine to discern. Nkem Nwankwo suggests this utter exploitation of time when he writes of music as that which "takes a small drop of the day and inflates it into a tempestuous sea in which the men and women drowned, that snatches from time one small moment and gives us the vastness of eternity." [8]

There is also in the diachronic structure of the music both an avoidance of the equivalent of skeletality and a disinclination to maximize the use of juncture for affecting effect. The use of juncture, of course, can as readily be a property of structure as of style, of time as of space. Skeletality is avoided by virtue of the fact that, although the music is not "visceral" or "fat"—it does not richly exploit a broad tonal spectrum—it is by no means spare. Its anatomy is not stressed for its own sake in order that all might perceive it and be affected by it. The music is, on the contrary, like a sinew—strong, kinetic, taut.

[8] Nkem Nwankwo, *Danda* (London: Andre Deutsch, 1964), p. 24.

132

The affecting use of juncture must, under such circumstances as I have given, be minimal, for juncture by definition is the boundary between two features such that—in our use here—the point of meeting or articulation is affectingly emphasized. Boundary phenomena can exist synchronously among musical voices as well as diachronically among serial features. In neither case, however, do they find dramatic statement. In no respect, in short, is the drive toward structural continuity consistently frustrated.

The synchronic musical constructions tend to exhibit marked inhibition of tonal spectrum, working, as it were, from a limited palette. That very characteristic Nwankwo speaks of, that interlocking quality which aborts the strong emphasis of boundary phenomena at points of articulation, also serves to diminish the clear definition of many instruments in concert uttering many different though, in accordance with the laws of the particular music, *related* tones. One finds here that same sinewed quality.

Once again we observe light modeling of the surface, not only of the synchronic inventions but of the diachronic structure as well—indeed of the total musical entity. We see, all told, the same maintenance of intensionality which characterized both sculpture and the dance.

The modes of existence of the affecting presence among the Yoruba are well defined and, for the late traditional period with which we are concerned, constant; and the para-aesthemes are intension and continuity of the part and intensive continuity of the whole. In summary, the para-aesthemes may be shown as in Table 7, with arrowheaded equal signs indicating the universe of their similetic equivalence.

The intensively continuous affecting presence among the Yoruba exists in these terms as a self-existent, ontologically independent, self-perpetuating, affecting act. I assert with confidence that the fundamental affect evidenced by these features, as I have seen them, is basic to the content of the cultural metaphoric base, to which intension and continuity are tropes. This basic mode has profound affecting value for the Yoruba, though certainly it is not a generalization which is consciously known to them. The principle of intensive continuity provides the necessary and sufficient metaphoric conditions for the expression and creation of what is profound and profoundly basic to their being.

Table 7. Model: Intensive Continuity as Expressed in Sculpture, Dance, Music

	SCULPTURE	DANCE	MUSIC
INTENSION	Avoidance of limbs, hands, and feet extending freely into space. All show a marked tendency to be bound to body and to earth.	Avoidance of referring expressive gestures to the extremities; concentration↔of affecting emphasis upon head-body↔leg core.	Avoidance of broad tonal range, elaborate distinction of tonal entities; closeness is asserted. Close "interlocking of events" in "cross-section" of time.
CONTINUITY	Assertion of long body lines; minimum of modeling; adjustment of normal body proportions to enhance columnar quality↔of body.	Assertion of continuity synchronically as sculpture does, diachronically 1) as part↔continuity of musical system, 2) as↔density of events in balletic time. Understatement of movements equivalent to minimum of modeling.	Assertion of maximal exploitation of musical time; very close sense of genetic development; de-emphasis of tonal exploitation in favor of emphasis of rhythm equivalent to light modeling.

It is difficult, if not indeed impossible, to find much by way of corroborating evidence to support my case. It is for that reason that I cite the following with particular pleasure, for it attests not only to what I have observed about music, but suggests the pervasiveness of a general principle of intensive continuity. Although not from a Yoruba but from a neighboring people, this reveals the presence of common views.

Dr. Donatus Nwoga, a University of Dublin Ph.D. currently with the English department in the University of Nigeria, Nsukka, visited with us in Benin last year. As we were playing some of our tapes for him, we began to discuss the special nature of African music and the problems involved in its esthetic judgment. In this regard he mentioned that once he was hanging pictures on the wall of his home while his father was visiting with him. His father told him: "You have become westernized, my son. You hang the pictures far apart from each other, leaving space in between. We like the pictures to be close to each other. We do not want to leave an empty space." Nwoga told us that this remark made him think about Ibo drumming. The musician, he said, does not want to leave an empty space between his beats. Whenever there is room a drummer will introduce a new rhythm which will fill the gaps around the dominant beat. The beauty of drumming results from this interlocking of rhythms.[9]

[9] I am indebted for this information to Professor Daniel Ben-Amos, who told me of it one evening after a discussion at the University of California at Los Angeles.

The Narrative and Intensive Continuity: The Palm-Wine Drinkard

Thus far I have been chiefly concerned with sculpture, a spatial form. Now, to broaden the base for understanding the mode of intensive continuity at work, it would be desirable to observe its effects in yet another dimension—time—discerning similetic equivalents at the levels of the objective and formal metaphors and ascertaining the existence of the para-aesthemic intensive continuity. I have chosen to treat narrative separately from the other forms for several reasons. In the first place, I am more at home with narrative than I am with the other forms, and thus I can produce a more detailed analysis. Certainly at least one such more fully analytical exposition would clearly be desirable.

I have elected to work with *The Palm-Wine Drinkard*,[1] a folk-fantasy by Amos Tutuola, rather than with the novels of Wole Soyinka or T. M. Aluko, simply because the novel is an imported phenomenon. Its mere exercise interposes a certain distance between practitioner and tradition, such that it becomes that much more difficult to see the traditional affecting principle at work in an alien form. That form is exotic and learned, and its very exercise implies a further degree of acculturation. At the very least, one cannot perceive the principle's effects with the

---

[1] Amos Tutuola, *The Palm-Wine Drinkard* (London: Faber and Faber Ltd., paper, 1962).

137

same sharpness of focus one can have in the case of the more traditional sub-forms (if narrative is the form, then "novel" and "short story" are sub-forms).

Prior to analysis, however, it is necessary for us to consider the media which comprise verbal narrative, discussing them in general and considering where we should expect continuity and discontinuity, intension and extension to be expressed in these media—situationality, language, relationality, and experience. Each of these media is to be seen as having both synchronic and diachronic dimensions existing both in instantaneity and in sequentiality.

Situationality

Situationality is that dimension of human activity which most readily comes to mind when narrative is mentioned, for when one is asked what a given narrative is "about" and proceeds to recount the plot, he is giving a synopsis of that narrative medium. Situation is composed of actor, action, motivation, sense detail, and psychological detail, and it exists as readily in the internal world of the individual actor as it does interpersonally. The properties of situation are inextricably related to one another in specific times and places and for specific reasons since there must be a logic—an entailment, a follow-through—about human action if it is not to be chaotic. There is a decreasing entropy of action with every action committed. Granting a situation where actor and action have no predictable or reasonable relationship one to the other, where motivation is irrelevant to action and to actor, and where sense and psychological details are either not significant or counter-significant to each of the other properties, it is doubtful whether meaningful narrative could exist. Of course, disjunctions among the properties may be used for special effect, and indeed surrealistic works may exist in which other logics prevail—such as the hidden logic of relationships among dream symbols. But in the first instance, such disjuncture does not characterize the total work, and in the second a logic does prevail, even if it is not the daily logic of fully disclosed cause and effect.

Situation is divisible into *acts,* which are identifiable, synchronic units constituting in their totality the medium of situationality in a given work. More specifically, an act is defined in terms of all the properties of situation, insofar as they are to be found within the span of situation under consideration, which conspire together to constitute an identifiable phase in the diachronic progression of the narrative. An act is recognized when it can be asserted that at a given time and in a given place such and such an event of dramatic import occurred.

Concerning the properties of situation, there are instances in narrative in which the distinction between sense detail and psychological detail would appear to be less than clear. Sense detail can be used for the purposes of providing psychological information, as when it is used to create mood or when it assumes significant or symbolic value by representing or conveying something of the state of mind of one of the actors. For the purposes of analysis, however, it would seem best to take such details as they are given rather than as they are intended. Sense and psychological details may be used to give extension to a synchronic act; or, indeed, they may restrict it, thus making the act intensive, much as the variously voiced instruments of a symphony orchestra may be used in wide or narrow range in order to extend or to restrict the synchronic structures of a given musical composition. Sense detail and psychological detail also contribute to the establishment of the durational existence of a work by maintaining continuity of scene and mood.

The psychological detail which is used to create the emotional milieu of a work, as sense detail creates its physical world, must be distinguished from the psychological elements of a character adduced to give depth—or not adduced, thus producing shallowness—and believability to the motivation which links together actor and action in any given act and indeed in any given sequence of acts. Motivation may be explicit or implicit, simple or complex, obvious or subtle, resident in present situations or in situations past or yet to come; and it may be rooted in one's self, in another, or in the interests of some event quite removed from either. Motivation is the seed of action, expressed or repressed, and as it constitutes the license for action, so, when it is believable, does it establish action's historicity and authenticity. Finally, for the properties of situation, there is little that need be said of actor and action since these properties would appear to be self-explanatory.

139

34. *Reclining female figure, Yoruba.*

Language

Language is the second medium of narrative, and it has several properties—denotation, connotation, images, irony, wit, paradox, ambiguity, rhythm, contrast, alliteration, sound, and the whole range of rhetorical devices which may be used to give fabric, meter, balance, and affect to the narrative—all these, of course, in addition to the common properties of language: tense, mood, voice, and case. Primarily, the affecting properties of language are useful in creating range of act, and thus they are chiefly of concern in the consideration of the problem of intensionality/extensionality. But in their duration and frequency, they are of relevance also in the consideration of continuity/discontinuity, such that any property or indeed any group of properties consistently employed constitutes an added stratum of durationality.

Relationality

By relationality, I mean synchronic relationships among components of acts as well as the durational ones among acts in sequence. In both cases, one is concerned with the consideration either of integration, by which the properties of situation and of language are functionally or causally—in any event, meaningfully—related one to the other, or of disintegration. It is characteristic of the continuous work that consequentiality characterizes the relationships among acts and larger patterns of acts; but such dependency does not characterize such relationships among acts in the discontinuous narrative although, obviously, it must at the very least govern the relationships among the constituent elements composing an act.

Experience

Experience is that flush of pertinence that characterizes an affecting presence and makes it valuable, intimate, and believed. One expects that the medium of experience will tend to be more or less implicit and centripetal in the intensive work and the opposite in the extensive one, that a constant state of evolving experience will characterize the continuous while a succession of estates of experience, doubtless unrelated, will characterize the discontinuous.

141

Modeling

Modeling, which is not, of course, an affecting medium but is nonetheless a critical factor in considering the style of a people, will be either high or low, with the former leading to fully individuated characters and situations developed with marked credibility, and the latter leading to characters' being portrayed as types, with their actions lacking something of both credibility and distinctiveness. Diachronically, in the case of high modeling, one sees characters develop and believes their change. This is less notably the case in low modeling. High synchronic modeling we would expect to characterize extensionality, and high diachronic modeling, continuity. Conversely, low synchronic modeling would be equivalent to intensionality and low diachronic modeling, to discontinuity.

It will be useful to present in schematic survey the characteristics of each of the media in intensionality and extensionality, in continuity and discontinuity. (See Table 8.)

There is, it must be noted, a difference between competence and lack of it, so that there is, in effect, excellence or failure in the practice of narrative, satisfaction or defect in the use of the media and their properties. Thus, when best executed the intensional character is subtle, but when less well realized he is shallow and unbelievable. Similarly, the extensional character at his best is complex and exciting, while at his worst he is disorganized, bombastic, hollow. The complexity of action or of language that characterizes the extensional is at best rich, and at worst rococo. The outward-tending, the reaching, in defect becomes mere disorganization; the intending, cramped; the subtle, shallow; the continuous, tiresome; and the discontinuous, chaotic.

As is sometimes true of models, they can reflect more entities than can in reality be readily found to exist. This is particularly the case with the question of continuity and discontinuity as it relates to narrative. That is, in narrative existing in language and language being characterized by certain demands of consecutivity, absolute discontinuity would not be possible. Taken at the level of the smallest meaningful isolable unit—the act—it is inconceivable that either one of the only two possibilities of discontinuity would exist. Either each act would be so explicitly defined and executed in such a way as to focus affective attention upon those acts themselves, at the expense of *before* and *after,* or sequentiality would be handled in such a way that no act would follow from any other act. As we shall see when we consider *The Palm-Wine Drinkard,* this argument has special relevance to the episodic work, the existence of which would be made problematic under the mode of continuity. It is probably the case that there is an *intention* toward continuity and an *intention* toward discontinuity which are made manifest in the work. If this is true, then it is in this area that we must search for continuity and for discontinuity. Once again, the discussion of Tutuola's work will make clear the evidences of such intentions in the case of a work which is episodic yet continuous, if not in terms of action, at least in terms of other affecting media and their properties.

Amos Tutuola's *The Palm-Wine Drinkard* is one of those marvelous works of the human imagination which, rich with fancy, goes simply and directly to the heart of a perennial and profound human concern—the nature of the estate of being dead. Although the story is inevitably and inextricably involved with Tutuola's being Yoruba, it is equally tightly bound to his being a man. Thus, the impact of much of what he writes is supracultural; the nature of the impact is of that special and very basic level of pertinence which one calls Myth. (I capitalize the term to distinguish it from that "myth" which the anthropologist sees culturally and whose function is to "validate" action.)

In *The Palm-Wine Drinkard,* Tutuola relates the adventures of a first-person narrator whose palm-wine tapster has been killed falling from a tree while tapping palm-wine. The victim of a prodigious appetite for palm-wine and a generous host who is deserted by his friends once he can no longer supply them with the hospitality to which they have become accustomed from him, he sets off to find his palm-wine tapster. "When I saw that there was no palm-wine for me again, and nobody could tap it for me, then I thought within myself that old people were saying that the whole people who had died in this world, did not go to heaven directly, but they were living in one place somewhere in this world. So that I said that I would find out where my palm-wine tapster who had died was" (p. 9).

This is not a "descent to the underworld" only because there is no underworld. The Town of the Deads is in the same world as the towns of the living. But in spirit, the mythic formula ob-

143

Table 8. Model: Media Characteristics of Narrative

	SYNCHRONIC		DIACHRONIC	
	Intensionality	Extensionality	Continuity*	Discontinuity
1. SITUATIONALITY *Sense detail*	There is an economy and close relevance to such sense detail as is included.	There is a richness to sense detail, and it may or may not be tightly integrated into the structure of act.	Sense detail is closely controlled diachronically with attention to warp, and woof being either lavish (extensive) or restrained (intensive).	Sense detail shows little evidence of supporting any notion of through-development.
Psychological detail	There is an economy and close relevance to such psychological detail as is included.	There is a richness to psychological detail, and such detail may or may not be tightly integrated into the structure of the act.	Psychological detail is closely controlled, and the development of the psychological dimensions of the work (mood) is evolutionary.	Psychological detail is loosely controlled. There is no sense of careful, evolutionary development of successive psychological details.
Motivation	Motivation is spare, pertinent, and closely integrated	Motivation is elaborately conceived and intricately extended to the periphery of the act.	Motivation is rigorously consequential and evolutionary.	Motivation is loosely consequential, or perhaps not consequential at all.
Action	Action is characterized by a strong focus, is definite and clear.	Action is complex, ranging, implicative.	Action is carefully consequential and evolutionary.	Action is sequential and tends to arrest forward movement.

	Intensionality	Extensionality	Continuity*	Discontinuity
Actor	The actor is well defined, executed with strong, clearly drawn lines.	The actor is richly drawn with a wealth of evocation, variety of motivation, complexity of personality (or simple personality completely, complexly shown).	The actor is developed in a carefully evolutionary fashion, such that all acts are logically derivable from previous conditions or referable to future ones.	The actor is loosely evolutionary or not evolutionary at all. He is seen stroboscopically rather than realistically through causal time.
2. RELATIONALITY	A narrow range of kinds of relationships among components of situation and other affecting media.	A wide range of kinds of relationships among components of situation and other affecting media.	Temporal integration is tight, and the principle of diachronic development is consequentiality. In the event of an episodic work, where sequentiality is apt to characterize the work, over-all evidences of integrative relationality will occur.	There is a sense of disjuncture among the parts such that sequentiality characterizes the work. The discontinuous episodic is not clearly overridden by larger, integrative plans.
3. LANGUAGE	Economical and rigorously pertinent use of images and other affecting properties of language so that the act is a tightly integrated synchronic event. Images tend to restrain the attention and focus the feeling.	Wide, indeed even lavish, use of images and other affecting properties of language so that act is a ranging affecting structure. Images are richly connotative and suggestive. Indefiniteness rules and implication and suggestion are vastly important.	Carefully integrative patterns of use of images and other affecting properties of language.	A disregard for the temporal *patterning* of images and other affecting properties of language.

*Continuity by means of a dense frequency of discrete "atoms" poses different considerations. See text.

tains, for the way to the Town of the Deads is fraught with har-rowing escapes from monsters who would destroy the narrator and, eventually, the wife whom he acquires in one of his earliest experiences, that with the "incomplete gentleman." There is no river Styx for him to cross, although at the end of his odyssey the narrator encounters the last monsters in a mountain just across a river, only seven miles from his own village. The bush in which the Deads' Town is located (years away from his own village) is, there can be little doubt, raised to the power of Myth. But this radically generalizing action comes perhaps more easily to the Yoruba than to the urban European, and more readily to the Yoruba of Tutuola's generation (Tutuola was born in 1920), per-haps, than to the "enlightened" young of today. For to the Yoruba, the bush has traditionally been a place of mystery and often of fear. One encounters again and again, in the fiction from the region, accounts of experiences and of beliefs which would indicate a certain awe toward the bush. Because of the Mythiza-tion of the bush, therefore, one might randomly expect to en-counter a functional equivalent of "crossing the Styx," and he is not disappointed. From the narrator's introduction—recount-ing his situation, the death of his tapster, and his determination to set forth in search—to the first adventures, there is a percep-tible boundary. The world of the introduction is a real world, except for the gargantuan appetites of the palm-wine drinkard, but the world of the first adventure is a world of the marvelous and the highly generalized. Thus his first experience takes him on a labor whose objective is the capture of Death.

Similar to other accounts of the world of the dead, the deads of Tutuola's bush do not care for the living. In fact, the living are not allowed in the Deads' Town, though the drinkard and his wife succeed in visiting there. The deads behave differently from the living also—notably, they walk backwards, which we are to read as a primitive form of behavior and the evidence for which is to be found in the section about the red people, where we learn that at one time people had their eyes on their knees and walked backwards. In the long run, the narrator learns that his trip was in vain. His tapster, once found, no longer wishes to return to the towns of the living. The tapster's transfiguration has been completed. He has visited some of the very towns the narrator himself has visited along the way, but having at last

146

reached Deads' Town his transformation into a dead is both complete and irreversible.

The narrator himself is by no stretch of the imagination an ordinary mortal. A person of enormous appetites, the palm-wine drinkard is more than somewhat gargantuan. When he begins his journey, he is careful to take along with him both his own and his father's juju, or power-containing substances. But the merit of this juju is not only to ward off evil; it is also used to effect basic physical transformations of himself, his wife, and their possessions. The juju is more that of the magician than of the ordinary man protecting himself against witchcraft. Unlike the ordinary mortal, furthermore, he can "sell" his death and "lease" his fear. And the first characterization he gives of himself, once he has launched himself into the bush of adventure, is as "father of the gods." One does not necessarily believe that this is in fact who he is, nor indeed that he himself takes this self-description fully seriously, although at one point at least he does appear to do so. He is, in some sense, very much like the hero in Greek myths. He is as generic as they, and like them he can—as generic—engage in those highly generalized experiences which have within them the conditions essential to becoming Myth. We shall see something more of this subsequently when we discuss his lack of individuation.

So a hero he is, and though his task may lack something of the dignity of purpose of Prometheus', his ultimate objective is nonetheless of social worth and to be viewed as heroic. After having spent years in the search of his tapster, when he reaches Deads' Town and locates his tapster, he takes back with him not the tapster but a gift—a miraculous egg which upon address will fulfill all that is asked of it. He returns home to find that a famine has settled upon the earth; and whereas he had undertaken his journey in order that he might supply both himself and the men of his village with palm-wine, he uses the magical powers of the egg to become the universal provider, defeating the famine and alleviating the hunger of all who come to his compound.

It is obvious that *The Palm-Wine Drinkard,* because it is of a given type, is reminiscent of other works in world literature. Gerald Moore is particularly aware of these similarities, for he specifically cites—in his discussion of Tutuola in *Seven African Writers*—Bunyan and Dante and likens the search of the palm-wine drinkard to that of Orpheus. But what distinguishes

148

36. *Silver elephant, Abomey, Fon.*

Tutuola's work from that of Bunyan and Dante is perhaps more significant than the similarities they share. Notably, *The Palm-Wine Drinkard* lacks anything of the sense of explicit moral purpose to which *Pilgrim's Progress* and *The Divine Comedy* are dedicated. Especially in contrast with the latter work, Tutuola's masterpiece is not dedicated to the purpose of summing up, as it were, a body of theological doctrine.

The two works with which *The Palm-Wine Drinkard* has most in common, though in very different ways, are the *Odyssey* and the *Canterbury Tales*. The *Drinkard* shares with the *Odyssey* many of its tale properties, notably the "descent" to the "underworld," wherein that special sense of the marvelous which characterizes the episodes of both Odysseus and the drinkard prevails. There are other points in common as well, chiefly a similarity of character; both Odysseus and the palm-wine drinkard live by the exercise of their cunning. But there is about the *Odyssey* a greater sense of the particular, and thus to some extent the mythic quality (which is always the more powerful the more nearly it approaches the general) of the *Odyssey* is less marked than that of *The Palm-Wine Drinkard*. Both these two works, and the *Canterbury Tales* as well, are similarly episodic, and they share in common the fact that each of them was written in a "popular" language. Chaucer wrote in English rather than in the French of the Court; Dante, in Italian rather than in Latin; and Tutuola, in a marked English dialect rather than in Yoruba or in the standard "literary" English his contemporaries learned in their colleges and universities. Further, Tutuola's work has an added feature in common with Chaucer's—an immediacy, a forthrightness, a freshness, and a keen sense of delight, a delight particularly to be seen in the common determination to underplay the touching, the outrageous, the amusing.

Chinua Achebe notes that "the English language will be able to carry the weight of my African experience. But it will have to be a new English, still in full communion with its ancestral home but altered to suit its new African surroundings." [2]

This, clearly, shows Tutuola's attitude toward and use of the English language. Yet his diction, which is that of the proletariat rather than that of the university graduate, has undoubtedly caused some among his contemporaries to deny him

[2] Chinua Achebe, "English and the African Writer," *Transition* 18 (1965): 30.

the great esteem he deserves as a major literary artist. Such persons have perhaps been "embarrassed" by his "illiteracies." In this respect, his publishers were kinder and more honest than some of his African critics. It was the personal decision of Sir Geoffrey Faber[3] that Tutuola's English should not be "normalized," thus permitting a work of major significance to reach the public in all the striking and often breathtaking originality of its prose.

In the long run, however, comparisons of one work with others, particularly when those works are from different cultures, are of limited utility. In the final analysis, any work must stand naked in its own terms before those who come face to face with it in affecting interaction. The greater its universal features—as contrasted with the ones which are appreciable only by those who are co-cultural with the work—the greater the extent to which the work will win international acceptance. This has been the case with Tutuola's book.

In any case, such evaluations, negative or positive, have as little to do with the grounds on which The Palm-Wine Drinkard is relevant to our present purposes as they do with the work itself. They constitute merely an interesting added dimension of context to the work's existence. What is of relevance here is solely that the work was created by a Yoruba and that it is in the narrative tradition of the Yoruba, a fact attested to by Ulli Beier, who points out that typical of the tradition is the use of "bizarre imagery," and the avoidance of moralizing and sentimentalizing. He also points out that in this last respect, in addition to drawing more heavily upon traditional folklore, Tutuola is more Yoruba than is Fagunwa, from whom it is asserted Tutuola has somewhat derived.[4] Tutuola further provides the student with a unique advantage—authentic Yoruba narrative "behavior" which is in many significant respects traditional, and yet he has doubly blessed the serious student who does not command enough of Yoruba to understand the traditional texts as they are traditionally communicated by writing in English! Tutuola's English is as authentic a presentation of the language uses of the Yoruba in the achievement of narrative as is a presentation in Yoruba. I assume that one's method of telling a story is the same whether

[3] Told to me through personal communication.
[4] Ulli Beier, "Fagunwa: A Yoruba Novelist," Black Orpheus 17 (1965): 52, 54.

151

he does it in one language or in a very different one. He will assert metaphors at the same kinds of places, similarly shape incidents, similarly proportion them and invoke their relationships, and will even tailor the second language somewhat—if he is not a master of its own idiom—along the stylistic lines of that mother tongue he more perfectly knows, much as he will shape the sounds of a second language to conform to the phonemes of his mother tongue.

This impressive fact, as well as the narrative's manifest and numerous other qualities notwithstanding, The Palm-Wine Drinkard has been rejected and maligned by those who should have been first to accept it—numerous of Tutuola's contemporaries, notably younger writers. Not only have they slighted the work on the basis of the normative considerations of grammar as indicated above, but they have also suggested that The Palm-Wine Drinkard is derivative. By such an observation, I suppose the intent has been somehow to demean the stature of the work. The sophisticated reader, however, jealously defends those works he values, and he is not to be put off by such observations. He knows there is much to be encountered in world literature that is borrowed. The envy or embarrassment of his contemporaries cannot hide the fact that Tutuola's work is rich with imagination (and if that imagination is the imagination of a people, to be encountered elsewhere in their works, it is then surely no less Tutuola's than anybody else's), incredibly inventive, superbly well told, touched with dignity and humor, with the poetic as well as the prosaic, with naiveté and with sophistication, with joy, with pathos, and with a strong appreciation of what is universal in the human condition.

At the other extreme of criticism, I have heard informed people criticize Tutuola because he has gone too far astray from the traditions of the oral tale as told by the Yoruba. Such people, typically Europeans and Americans, feel that Tutuola has not done the traditional tale well because he has not done it "properly."

Even so, the work reflects acculturation. Thus, its relationship to the traditional narrative is more nearly the relationship of Lamidi Fakeye, a contemporary carver who works in the tradition but with marked innovations, to the history of Yoruba art than it is that of young sculptors trained at university to work in the idioms of Europe to that same history. For those, while doubt-

152

37. Ram's head, Beni

less influenced by the Yoruba tradition, are consciously and more greatly influenced by Europe. It is more nearly the relationship of a village drummer to the mainstream of Yoruba music than it is that of the music of the modern, symphonic composer, like Fela Sowande, to that same tradition. Tutuola's relationship to the tradition of narrative is thus that of Fakeye to his carving and the traditional drummer to his music; the counterparts of the modern sculptor and Sowande are "university" writers, preeminently exampled by Wole Soyinka.

That one searches for Yoruba features in Tutuola's work indicates that what I have said is taken for granted by scholars in the field, that is, that he is of the tradition but acculturated. Beier's writing of "more Yoruba" and "less Yoruba" as between Tutuola and Fagunwa is a case in point. So is the essay of Bernth Lindfors, a work of admirable scholarly imagination which shows the common presence in contemporary Yoruba rhetoric of certain traditional devices, notably of a "string of hyperboles, the concern with number and amount, the climactic contrast."[5] Lindfors also lists as a feature of the traditional rhetoric the use of long strings of appositives and the enumeration of many items, which he calls "inventories."

In gross examination, the most immediately notable feature of *The Palm-Wine Drinkard* is its linear structure composed of segments of action which are more or less independent of one another. These segments constitute separate stories, so lacking is any sense of contingency or geneticity in their interrelationships. With respect to one another, then, these segments are more accurately to be characterized as sequential rather than consequential. They are, however, contingently related to the basic condition of the story, which is the search by the drinkard for his palm-wine tapster. There is little doubt, therefore, that the work is episodic.

The episodes of the story are of three kinds: those which involve fantastic monsters who attempt to victimize the protagonist —but are always defeated; those which are almost pastoral; and

---

[5] Bernth Lindfors, "Characteristics of Yoruba and Igbo Prose Styles in English" (paper given at Contemporary African Literatures seminar, held at the annual meeting of the Modern Language Association of America, New York, December 27, 1968), p. 5.

those which constitute the frame of the narrative. The first class of episodes tends toward the bizarre, the second toward the idyllic, and the third toward what we must accept as the "real" world. "The Complete Gentleman" sequence, an example of the first class, concerns a woman (later the drinkard's wife) captivated by a handsome man whom she follows home only to learn that he is naught but a skull who has borrowed the various parts of his body and must return them. The sequence in the white tree with the Faithful Mother is one of the two developed idyllic interludes, and it provides the drinkard and his wife with an opportunity for happiness and security—respite from the awful experiences they have already endured and are yet to undergo. Episodes of the frame, and frequent allusions to the chief dramatic purpose of the story, which the frame represents, taken together constitute the dramatic center of gravity for the work. The two other kinds of episodes are constellar, dramatic forces which play about that center of gravity, endowing the total structure with a rhythm of the three forces.

The action of the story is thus constituted of discrete segments, and, as far as concerns the protagonist, these segments almost wholly comprise the reactions of the drinkard to situations which have not been brought about as a result of anything he himself has done, except insofar as he made the initial decision to seek and subsequently to persist in his search for his palm-wine tapster. Although the episodes are not genetically related one to the other, neither are they genetically derived from the actions, the personality, or the free will of the protagonist. This leads to a narrative in which the protagonist persists outside of a dramatic framework described by the exercise of self and free will. As a result, at the mercy of the inevitable encounter with bizarre and primarily evil forces which dominate the land where his adventures take him, he is subjected to events which are structurally of radically limited kinds. However, such limitation does not describe the substantive nature of the experiences he undergoes, for all that he endures is varied and richly inventive. The universe within which the palm-wine drinkard exists, then, is one characterized by acts which result not from his being but from his circumstance, acts exerted upon him and to which he responds, and acts which are generically limited even though substantively varied. In a world where the protagonist cannot do as he will but as he must, the range of kinds of actions is

155

limited and the cause of the protagonist's actions is external to himself.

Existence in a world of limited possibilities, most of which amount to a threat to the individual's well-being, and where free will is irrelevant to all that happens to one, such existence entails a one-dimensionality of actor. Where not action but reaction is the rule, the scope of motivation is necessarily severely limited; and where what befalls one is universally physical, the development of character interiority is significantly restricted, if indeed it exists at all. The simultaneous operation of these two factors produces actors to match the world in which they find themselves—wooden beings subject to circumstance, victims rather than masters of their fate.

Perhaps it is not necessarily the case that characters who are primarily reactive lack something of believability, but this is markedly true in *The Palm-Wine Drinkard*. Since there is no significant development of the interiority of characters, psychological detail is radically limited. Even where the narrator does acknowledge fear, that fear is asserted rather than created in prose. The actors are one-dimensional, stimulus-response creatures living in a story world whose apparatus works neatly and inevitably, with precision, without ambiguity, in a world where clean action is all. It follows that the motivation which takes the actors from one action to the next is minimal, simple, and obvious, involving the preservation of one's self and the reduction of his needs. Further, the actors exist and the story is enacted within a bizarre world which exists minimally in description and is not at all constituted in the work. Chiefly, this world exists only because we are presented with assertions that a particular bizarre creature has appeared, or that an exotic condition of climate or of scene prevails. Even such assertions are rare, and we can thus readily conclude that scene, to the notably limited extent to which it is evoked, is not made integral to the story, and that it does not in any meaningful or believable sense exist. In the first instance, it is intension by default; and in the second, it is contributory as a stratum to the continuity of the work.

Language is marked by assertion rather than by connotation, and by description rather than by enactment. This latter characteristic would seem almost inevitable in view of the absence of any development of interiority and of sense and psychological detail. Imagistic devices are seldom used, and there is little evidence of any exploitation of the connotative edges of words, those which suggest color texture. What is most notable is the exploitation of speed—though this is more properly to be considered a function of the pacing of actions rather than of language —a keen sense for the bizarre invention, and a propensity toward incredible precision, particularly in matters of quantity, size, and price, which is often very humorous. Thus the drinkard asserts: "So my father gave me a palm-tree farm which was nine miles square and it contained 560,000 palm-trees, and this palm-wine tapster was tapping one hundred and fifty kegs of palm-wine every morning, but before 2 o'clock p.m., I would have drunk all of it; after that he would go and tap another 75 kegs in the evening, which I would be drinking till morning" (p. 7). Further, he asserts, his wife ". . . used the canoe as 'ferry' to carry passengers across the river, the fare for adults was 3d (three pence) and half fare for children. In the evening time, then I changed to a man as before and when we checked the money that my wife had collected for that day, it was £7: 5: 3d" (p. 39). The total they make for the month is £56: 11: 9d. As for the physical description, note the following:

As we were going further, we did not travel more than one third of a mile on this riverbank, before we saw a big tree which was about one thousand and fifty feet in length and about two hundred feet in diameter. This tree was almost white as if it was painted every day with white paint with all its leaves and also branches. As we were about forty yards away from it, there we noticed that somebody peeped out and was focusing us as if a photographer was focusing somebody (p. 65).

This striking image of the photographer "focusing" the drinkard and his wife is one of the very few explicit imagistic devices in the entire narrative.

Yet this use of quantification to the point of spurious accuracy constitutes a kind of "metaphoric" (in the traditional, literary sense) device; and although the more traditional classes of such devices are rarely to be encountered, this one of spurious accuracy is rife and rich. There is an effective difference of metaphor function that must be noted in passing, however. Whereas images are traditionally used in Western literature to suggest something of the nature of the unusual by creating some of its parameters in metaphor and simile, here by means of spurious accuracy the bizarre is made discrete and familiar in this

strange world Tutuola has created for us. The image is therefore in fact a kind of anti-image.

This use of the precise hyperbole is to be seen as an expression of the drive toward concreteness, and it is, one suspects, a traditional Yoruba narrative device. Certainly it is used equally by Tutuola and Fagunwa, as Lindfors demonstrates with the following excerpt from *The Forest of a Thousand Daemons:*

> My name is Akara-ogun, Compound-of-Spells, one of the formidable hunters of a bygone age. My own father was a hunter, he was also a great one for medicines and spells. He had a thousand powder gourdlets, eight hundred *ato,* and his amulets numbered six hundred. Two hundred and sixty incubi lived in that house and the birds of divination were without number. It was the spirits who guarded the house when he was away, and no one dared enter that house when my father was absent—it was unthinkable.[6]

The precise hyperbole is not only quantitative, however. Tutuola (and Fagunwa as well) resorts also to visual hyperbole, as indeed he must if he is to communicate the bizarre creatures which inhabit his forests. But it is something more than the fact of necessity that one notes in Tutuola's writing—it is a positive delight in the astounding invention. Here is the famous description of the Red Fish from *The Palm-Wine Drinkard:*

> . . . its head was just like a tortoise's head, but it was as big as an elephant's head and it had over 30 horns and large eyes which surrounded the head. All these horns were spread out as an umbrella. It could not walk but was only gliding on the ground like a snake and its body was just like a bat's body and covered with long red hair like strings. It could only fly to a short distance, and if it shouted a person who was four miles away would hear. All the eyes which surrounded its head were closing and opening at the same time as if a man was pressing a switch on and off (pp. 79–80).

Such devices deliver us into a world of hard concreteness and sharp definition, one that is an intensive universe of discrete entities. But it is interesting to note that clarity of delineation and physical individuation do not have actional counterparts. The most bizarre monster acts *generically,* in much the same way that is expected of any monster. The monster is thus in no sense individuated in terms of his own, unique monster-ness. What is achieved by this drive toward precision and concreteness of the

---

[6] Daniel O. Fagunwa, *The Forest of a Thousand Daemons: A Hunter's Saga,* trans. Wole Soyinka (London: Thomas Nelson & Sons, Ltd., 1968), p. 9.

3. *Chi-wara, Bambara.*

physical world is the evocation of the *category* of the specific rather than the specific itself. The affecting result of this process is that the unique is physically but not affectingly realized. On the contrary, it is the power of the general that is invoked. This produces a kind of paradox, and this paradox is a category of devices properly to be considered under the heading of the inhibition of range in the affecting medium of language in narrative.

The dramatic result of paradox is tension, and there is a system of such paradox-derived tensions in *The Palm-Wine Drinkard*. Take, for example, the situation near the end of the book where the drinkard is chased by the mountain-creatures. In order to escape, the drinkard

> . . . changed my wife into the wooden-doll as usual, then I put it into my pocket, and they saw her no more.
>
> But when she had disappeared from their presence they told me to find her out at once and grew annoyed by that time, so I started to run away for my life because I could not face them to fight at all. As I was running away from them, I could not run more than 300 yards before the whole of them caught me and surrounded me there; of course, before they could do anything to me, I myself had changed into a flat pebble and was throwing myself along the way to my home town (pp. 116–17).

The paradox involved in transforming one's wife and possessions into something one can carry, subsequently changing one's self into a pebble, and then throwing one's self is that between the probable and the improbable, the possible and the impossible which typically occurs in the book. Further, there is the paradox which results when the discrete meets the universal, a situation which prevails when the drinkard encounters "Dance," "Drum," and "Song," who aid him in his troubles with his monstrous son. "When 'Drum' started to beat himself it was just as if he was beaten by fifty men, when 'Song' started to sing, it was just as if a hundred people were singing together . . ." (p. 38). Subsequently, he encounters "Band," and "Spirit of Prey." Although these are somewhat different phenomena in that they are not "Platonic" abstractions, they meet "images" of themselves and personifications of "Land" and "Heaven." The structure of these encounters running through the story creates a rhythmic counterpoint to the total structure, providing a dynamic factor of some importance.

160

Involved in these paradoxes is the affecting medium of relationship, for paradox implies contradiction and contradiction
cannot exist without parts in inter-relationship. Paradox is to
be conceived of as a relationship in range, rather than in duration, and as previously mentioned, its intent is to establish dynamics of tension. But because the terms of the paradoxes exist
within the boundaries of a wildly improbable and circumstantial
universe where the extraordinary is ordinary, their impact is
by no means as great as it would be were they to appear in a
more orderly, more "logical" context.

This is true also of the relationships which cement the work
into a durational whole. Facts are not always related only in
terms of simple cause-effect relationships. The Faithful Mother
in the white tree is a sister of the Red King, but the Red King
asserts that his whole family, indeed all his people, were turned
red and sent to the place where they now reside. Now there is
no mention of the Faithful Mother's being red, and so we assume
she is not, for such an extraordinary fact would have been mentioned by Tutuola, who never fails to note the outlandish whenever it is possible to do so. On the other hand, neither are we
given the circumstances under which she became other than red.

Those numerous instances in which the drinkard is threatened
with death also fall under this a-causal relationship. He knows,
as well as do his readers, that it is, as he often reminds himself,
impossible for him to die since he has sold his death. Thus, the
threat of death is meaningless to him. The situation is not wholly
reduced by the fact that he did not sell his fear, and thus is yet
able to be afraid, for he yet seems to entertain the prospect of
death as a reasonable one. There are numerous instances in
which actions are joined one to the other by means of relationships which defy the ordinary logic of the orderly procedure of
human action.

Intension/Extension

We are here concerned with the question of range in *The Palm-
Wine Drinkard*. If there is noticeable range in the situationality,
language, relationality, and experience of the work, it is extensive, whereas if the opposite is true, it is intensive.

When considering range as an inventory of classes of situations
and kinds of action-actor patterns, we have already noted that

there are three classes of actions which occur in the narrative: those which constitute the frame of the work, those which are idyllic, and those predominating ones which involve experiences with monsters. Even if we remove some of the generalization involved in this last and most numerous category, removing the consideration from so structural a level and glimpsing something of the particularities of experience, we see that there is little of significant differentiation among the episodes with the monsters. The monster is always physically remarkable, always threatening to the welfare of the narrator, always outwitted by the narrator. The pattern of action-actor relationships is such that the protagonist responds preponderantly to actions initiated by agents other than himself.

The actors themselves also exhibit markedly limited variety. There are both good and evil characters, but there is no significant moral shading. As a result, none of them is morally problematic. Their motivations are of limited variety as well, involving primarily action from the monsters and reaction from the narrator and his wife. The use of details of sense and psychology in scene and character creation is so minimal that there is little point even to mentioning it here.

The situation is not markedly different for language. Only one kind of "imagistic" device is typically used, that of the precise hyperbole which we have described as an anti-image. Diachronic relationships tend to display greater variety than is characteristic of the other media; for in durational terms, cause begets adequate and predictable effect in many instances, but in others, it does not. Examples of the first sort are commonplace, and even those of the second are numerous. But perhaps these latter ones require an example or two since they are much less common in narrative. One a-causally related eventuation occurs when the narrator and his wife produce a monster for a child, who grows to maturity within days and, outstripping his parents, relegates them to the role of servants. So also are the relationships among the various episodes a-causal. These relationships contrast with even the most remarkable of the other types of events in the narrative; as bizarre as they might be, they yet are rooted in causality, either in the power of the narrator's juju (such as the magical transformations) or in the nature of the peculiar laws of the spiritual world of the bush (the strange habits of the deads).

The synchronic dimension of relationality lacks careful definition and integration. There is thus no necessary relationship
between the kinds of monstrosity, of which there is great variety
if not great range, and the kinds of actions those monsters com-
mit. Neither is particularity of place related to the kind of action
which occurs, nor even is the general place (i.e., the bush of
monsters and the Town of the Deads), because the prodigious,
the strange, and the magical happen as readily in the "real"
world of the protagonist's village as they do in the bush of monsters and the Town of the Deads. In short, there is no close exploitation of relational integration such as one would expect of
the intensional work; but on the other hand, neither is there the
complexity or richness of relationality one would expect to find
in the extensive work.

Finally, concerning the medium of experience—which has
been defined in terms of its relevance to man and his human
condition—one can assert only that it is limited, for there is
little universality in the affairs of the drinkard. Raised to the level
of Myth, however, the search takes on rich significance for every
man.

Range also can be understood in terms of the "spread" of
given instances of the above items, as opposed to their taxonomy.
In this connection, range is inhibited in nearly every case,[7] with
the sole exceptions occurring in two areas. The first of these is
the richness of invention applied to the devising of the physical
and behavioral characteristics of the monsters and the deads
and the prolific use of the images of discreteness. There is thus
in this latter respect a certain amount of extensiveness—of
spread—to the medium of language; although, as we have suggested, since this "spread" is in the direction of concreteness,
its net effect is intensive. The second area is the use of language;
and since it tends to create a world of the particulate and is used
toward the ends of invention rather than of imagination—of
artifice rather than of constituting experience—it has its focus
on the discrete, the specific, the quantified, and the evaluated.
There is in Tutuola's work a drive toward precision and clarity,
despite its substantive fantasy. The inhibition of imagination,
connotation, and evocation is an exercise in the direction of the
reduction of ambiguity and is thus an exercise in intension.

[7] See the outline of the features of range of these various respects in Table 8.

164

There is, in short, range in invention if not in imagination—as the term is defined here.

Otherwise, the draft of the media is shallow. For situation, actions reach but feebly and without marked penetration into the depths of possibility in subtlety, variety, richness of experience, and in the exercise of the human fancy. Motivation is neither profound nor revealing; and the actors, largely because of these factors, are one-dimensional, even though lively. Not only is there little development at all of the physical world within which actions occur, but there is not even the careful elaboration of its properties. There is present in the work a radical inhibition of the complexity of causality. As a result, there neither can be any significant range to relationality. Language, as we have said, denotes rather than connotes.

The philosophical framework within which the work exists is one characterized by the proscription of the exercise of free will. The narrator persists in a world in which he has no choice over what happens to him. But since he endures by his own free will at least, even though in a world where freedom of will is abrogated, he submits to a moral order that is one of imposed and unpredictable outrage. In this world in which free will does not exist, only limited evil can happen—the protagonist cannot die, for example. It is a world in which planned, logical, and genetic action is severely limited, if not impossible. The revocation of free will must be seen as the sufficient cause of the action-reaction pattern described earlier as well as of the absence of the meaningful development of motivation. The inhibition of the possibility of doing as one chooses restricts the volitional world, shrinking the world of will almost to the point of non-existence. That actions happen to the protagonist does not alter the situation, both because of the limited variety of those actions and because no matter how varied they might conceivably be, such variety would not change this fact about the moral universe of the work.

The philosophical nature of *The Palm-Wine Drinkard*, the restriction of range in situation (and its properties of scene, actor, action, motivation), in language, and in relationality—all bespeak the influence of a strong drive toward intension in the execution of narrative. Elements which would tend to make acts extensive are avoided—the connotative values of words, the use of imagination as opposed to invention, full-dimensioned characters

166

41. Bronze mask, Benin

rather than types, and a full spectrum of human motivations and actions.

Continuity/Discontinuity

The absence of geneticity of relationality characterizes the durational dimension of *The Palm-Wine Drinkard,* which is thus episodic, and, in effect, discontinuous. If this is true, then narrative, in this respect, negates the mode of continuity we have hypothesized for it—as indeed it negates the argument of this book—for we have maintained the existence of an affecting system of similetic equivalents as a condition of a homogeneous culture. We have assumed that late, traditional Yoruba culture has such homogeneity, at least in relation to the affecting presence in it.

But the relevant question now is whether it is the discontinuity between episodes which is affectingly important, or whether it is that episodicism itself. The former would appear to be false by the test of system (which is the case in the other forms), while the latter would appear to be affirmed by the same test. In the other affecting forms, we have seen continuity asserted not in the way typical of Europeans and Americans—by means of long lines of through-development—but rather atomistically; for in the temporal works of the Yoruba, continuity can be seen as a function of the density of multiple, discrete parts. Continuity as a function of a high frequency of discrete integers can be achieved in narrative only by means of the episodic; and in order to come into being, the episodic requires a certain amount of disjuncture with respect to the relationships among its components and their immediate contexts.

Looked at somewhat differently, the situation amounts to this: we cannot regard the discontinuity of episodicism as an important feature in its own terms, since discontinuity defines the conditions under which episodicism may be said to exist. Were we to stress that discontinuity is of critical import, we would have to deny the possibility of creating an episodic work to those who in their affecting works assert the mode of continuity. We would therefore have to run the risk of denying the possibility of much of oral literature, for it is obvious that the conditions of oral tale-telling are favorable to the generation of the episodic. *The Palm-Wine Drinkard,* then, achieves continuity through density, in much the same way as the discrete beats of drumming occur with such dense frequency as to create a temporal "solid," or continuity.

This, I think, is the most important evidence in support of the continuity in Tutuola's work, and it thus defends the integrity and ultimately the reality of the system described. There is other evidence, however. There are, in the work, certain constants which clearly indicate a drive toward continuity. At least five of these constants can be readily identified.

1. The constancy of the improbable. The total, durational fabric of the work is characterized by a markedly high frequency of appearance of the remarkable, the wondrous, the unlikely—the improbable, in short.

2. The constancy of the permanence of the narrator—not only the constancy of point of view as a technical device of executing the narrative, but also, and indeed primarily, the constancy of the dramatic value of knowing that the protagonist, having sold his death, is bound to endure.

3. The constancy of the generalized character of the event. We have adequately discussed this point elsewhere in connection with the absence of individuation.

4. The constancy of the contrast between the real world of the reader and the fanciful one of the narrative. This is perhaps best regarded as the equivalent in scene of the improbability of event discussed under the first entry above.

5. The constancy of the frame. It is above all the unity of protagonist and of purpose which demonstrates the narrative's drive toward continuity.

But continuity through density is achieved not only by means of the episodic characteristics of the work. There is a noticeable drive toward the proliferation of entities, which gives further support to the view that, with respect to duration, the aesthetic of the Yoruba is expressive of the atomistic approach to continuity. Doubtless this is conditioned by the predominance of percussive instruments in music, which (except for the pressure drum) cannot sustain sound, and by the basically oral nature of the narrative, including *The Palm-Wine Drinkard*—of which it may justifiably be maintained that the fact that it is written is purely accidental to its nature.

How else does one explain the frequency of the precise hyper-

169

bole? Is it only a non-functional, decorative element found as a characteristic of the execution of the language of Yoruba narrative, or does one assume on the contrary that there is some reason for having opted for this out of all possible kinds of images —indeed out of all kinds of hyperbole? Reason would seem to argue in support of the latter alternative, and when Tutuola says that the drinkard consumes seventy-five barrels of palmwine of an evening rather than "some," or "a great quantity," or even "barrels," the atomistic aspect of the situation is stressed —Tutuola is searching for the proliferation of entities, composing the situation of its bits and pieces and calling attention to them.

It is doubtful, given the nature of the content of the narrative, whether one can maintain that the invention of the story, essential as it is to create the bizarre with which the story is concerned, reflects in any direct way the imperative toward atomistic density. Yet one cannot help but note that there seems to be a kind of special interest in the particulateness of the monsters' enormities, so inventively are they made, so lovingly are they noted. The description of the Red Fish, quoted earlier above, provides a good example.

An excellent instance of the interest in the particulate is to be seen in the following: "My wife had said of the woman we met: 'She was not a human-being and she was not a spirit, but what was she?' She was the Red-smaller-tree who was at the front of the bigger Red-tree, and the bigger Red-tree was the Red-king of the Red-people of Red-town and the Red-bush and also the Red-leaves on the bigger Red-tree were the Red-people of the Red-town in the Red-bush" (p. 83, punctuated thus). It is difficult to doubt that in this passage, which is perhaps the most remarkable one, in terms of our discussion, in the entire work, Tutuola takes delight in being as specific as he can, in maximizing every opportunity to give to his prose a density of discrete reference which indeed is contributory to *constituting* the mode of continuity in the work.

The "drumming" feature of the contemporary Yoruba popular prose style has been mentioned elsewhere. Ulli Beier says of Fagunwa, "He is a master of rhetoric, who can make repetitions and variations swing in a mounting rhythm, like Yoruba drumming."[8] One notes this same characteristic in Tutuola—in the

[8] Beier, "Fagunwa," p. 53.

170

passage quoted immediately above, in the pace of his inventions, in the rhythm of his actions, and in his regulation of pace with the diminuendo effect brought about by the inclusion of idyllic interludes. But the work of Tutuola is like drumming in more respects than these, for the narrative exists in terms of its properties of situation and language, its system of tensions, its relationality, the contrasts between its world and the world of the reader, between the general and the specific, the probable and the improbable. These various voices, like the voices of different drums, assert their own drives toward continuity, producing an interwoven structure by contributing their strata of particulate reality to the general density by which the continuity of the narrative is constituted.

All that *The Palm-Wine Drinkard* aesthetically *is* can be accounted for by that network of synapses and interstices (which feeling ultimately fills in) composed of the nerves of media and properties that have been identified. The affecting reality of the work is this, and nothing more. Who wrote it, under what circumstances, his role in society, the identity and social placement of his readers, their opinions of the work as to its quality, originality, and impact—all such considerations, while of undoubted import in other considerations, are irrelevant here.

The Palm-Wine Drinkard actualizes the Yoruba aesthetic as it has been described here, owing its affecting existence to the discipline of those same principles of intensive continuity that characterize the other forms of the affecting presence. To be sure, intensive continuity has determined the nature of the narrative's media in ways proper to narrative.

Those conditions of the affecting media which express or execute intension, as well as those which express or execute continuity, are aesthemes. The contributions these aesthemes make toward the systemic whole are such that we may speak of intension and continuity as para-aesthemes of the part and of intensive continuity as the para-aestheme of the whole, even more surely than we could after examining sculpture, dance, and music. The aestheme of the whole in *The Palm-Wine Drinkard* is obviously that confluence of the expression of intension and continuity in such a way that the work may be demonstrated to exhibit intensive continuity.

There can be no doubt that Amos Tutuola is closer to the traditional aesthetic of the Yoruba than are those of his con-

172

temporaries who have turned to the novel. This is a relative estate at best, to be sure, for the traditional culture has been heavily acculturated. One would expect upon further study, therefore, to perceive a continuum of "Yoruba-ness," extending from Tutuola at the deeply Yoruba end to Wole Soyinka at the more Europeanized, modernized end, with T. M. Aluko standing somewhere in between.

Raised to the cultural level, at least as far as concerns those writers publishing in English, one would expect to explain, in terms of the suasion of the traditional aesthetic, many of the characteristic "flaws" or "shortcomings" Europeans often appear to see in the West African practice of narrative. Thus, episodicism is the affecting desire to achieve continuity by means of a density of discrete elements rather than by the attenuation of long lines of dramatic—actional, psychological—development. "Shallowness" of draft, lowness of modeling in the delineation of characters and of scene development, can be seen as the exercise of the imperative to achieve intensivity, on the one hand, and as the drive toward the generalized presentation of character, the concern with the type, the role, on the other.

All West African, English-speaking writers show these characteristics to one degree or another, and that critic who fails to take into account the operation of the imperatives of an aesthetic *system* at the unconscious, cultural level practices the art of criticism irresponsibly. One can only wonder what innovations might have been wrought in the perpetration of narrative if the writers of West Africa had pursued and developed their craft in accordance with the dictates of their traditional aesthetic.

A Note on the Affecting Presence in Jogjakarta

The affecting works of the Yoruba, and of Guinea Coast Africa in general, are expressive of intensive continuity. It may be useful, by way of contrast, to present a sketch of the affecting presence in its various forms with a people who express an opposing principle of affecting reality—the Javanese, who have elected the metaphoric system of extensive discontinuity. Although on a large scale there are no major differences, to any but the most practiced observer, among the peoples of the various regions of Java (as, for example, there would be between the Javanese and the Yoruba), in the narrow scale of the anthropologist the differences that exist tend to become significant. Thus, I must specifically state that among the Javanese, the people of Jogjakarta are those with whom I shall be concerned.

Jogjakarta lies in south-central Java not far from Solo, where *Homo soloensis* was discovered. Like Solo, Jogjakarta is, and has been for centuries, a rich capital. In contrast to that of the cities of Nigeria, its recorded history is great, extending back through the recent colonial period to periods of Islamic, Hindu, and Buddhist influences. Jogjakarta has a population somewhere near 300,000. Its people, who are predominantly Moslem, make their livings chiefly as small manufacturers, shopkeepers, artisans, administrators, and landowners.

Dance, drama, costumery, music, and sculpture have long

174

characterized the area, and as the presence of a royal court of great splendor would suggest, these have been vigorously and indeed elaborately developed. This long history of the affecting presence notwithstanding, the discussion here will relate to the traditional affecting presence as it was encountered in 1957, taking the past into account for the purpose of providing historical depth as required. Thus, from the evidence of the abundant bas-reliefs in the ancient temples, it seems that the dance has changed little in a millennium. Then, as now, the dancer refers his expressive gestures to the extremities of his body, to the head, the hands, and the feet—indeed even to the wagging of the head in salute, the expressive uses of the eyes, the postures of the fingers and toes as they extend into space.

Each movement of the dance appears to be maximally extended into space—arms are extended, a leg is raised and the knee bent, the great toe is thrust upwards, and the fingers are curved and posed. I make the qualification "appears to be" because, quite naturally, not every movement is likely to be maximally extended if the dance itself is to be characterized by interesting and supple dynamics, as is indeed the case with the dance of Jogjakarta; the expressive movements are referred as extensively into space as is consistent with the dramatic import of the affect being conveyed. Heretofore, the acceptable fashion of the dance was called *halus,* and its characteristic lay not in extension but rather in consideration of the attitude with which that extension was accomplished. Extension was executed delicately, smoothly, flowingly. Later, however, another fashion was introduced. Called *kasar,* it emphasizes vigor in the assertion of extensionality. The arms and the legs intrude quickly and indeed even violently into space, with the effect that extensionality is even more dramatically asserted than it previously was (and for that matter still is, since the *halus* is still the favored fashion of dancing).

As the body synchronically exhibits much in common with the presentation of the body in movement as seen in the temple reliefs, so also does it in the diachronic dimension of the dance. The reliefs proceed by narrative, presenting one scene after the other, as does any series of narrative reliefs. It is striking, however, that the body in dance should, in its dance development, present much the same impression as the narrative series of the reliefs, for the dancer does not gradually, flowingly emerge,

175

with marked illusion of continuity, from one movement or position into the next. Quite to the contrary, the sense of the scene is accentuated. The diachronic development of the dance resembles the panels of the reliefs. The performer executes one movement with careful definition, and then, with a great sense of the individuality of the execution of that movement, the next is executed, equally studiedly. The temporal development of the dance emphasizes the serial aspect of the structure, with a resulting emphasis upon the discreteness of the parts.

The puppets of Jogjakarta must stand as the representative of sculpture since recently there has not been any notable practice of sculpture; indeed, Claire Holt quotes Sir Thomas Stamford Raffles as saying that "the art of sculpture had been completely lost" at the time of his lieutenant-governorship of Java (1811–16).[1] These puppets, however, exhibit characteristics of presentation identical to those of the reliefs and of the dancers. Constructed of either leather (two-dimensional) or wood (three-dimensional), the puppets respectively are used for shadow plays and for direct performance. The puppets, or *wayang*, are uniformly grotesque (figs. 8, 9), although the leather ones are more notably so than the wooden ones. The presence not only of exaggerated extensionality, but also of pronounced attention to the joints of the limbs, so that the continuous aspect of the extension of the body in space is de-emphasized, is of particular interest and is observed with the *wayang kulit* (leather puppets). If it is not the case that discontinuity is created, then at least that same interest in discontinuity we have perceived diachronically in the dance is here similetically expressed in a way possible in terms of the nature of the organism. A leg or an arm cannot of course *in fact* be discontinuous; but by emphasizing the joints and angles of legs and arms, one creates a functional substitute for discontinuity via the interruption of continuity, and he creates a similetic equivalent of the seriality of the diachronic forms.

In contrast to the Yoruba, who assert the frontality of the body, the Jogjanese assert its laterality. They are most interested in presenting the body in outline, a natural function of asserting the values of extensionality and discontinuity. This avoidance of frontality has several interesting consequences. In the first

[1] Claire Holt, *Art in Indonesia: Continuities and Change* (Ithaca: Cornell University Press, 1967), p. 192.

place, it explains why the Javanese developed the puppet play behind a screen (wayang kulit), where only the outline of the body—indeed the outline of the trees and buildings of the environment as well—is significant. In the second place, it makes understandable the strange sense of two-dimensionality one experiences in interpersonal relationships, for, as an outsider, one has the feeling he is never engaging fully with a total person. The Jogjanese act with great reserve toward the outsider, universally exhibiting a markedly uniform public personality.[2] It is as though they, too, were showing upon the screen of public occasion only the shadows of themselves.

The dance costume, as well as the costume elements carved on the Wayang puppets, reveals the drive toward extensional discontinuity and two-dimensionality. Costume comprises basically an ankle-length batik garment, an elaborate headdress, and sometimes a quiver for arrows (bows, arrows, and knives are the most common accouterments of costume). Around the waist is a long piece of cloth which is of great importance in gesture and in the execution of dance movements, since it is sometimes flicked here, flicked there, or momentarily permitted to rest upon the hand. The headdress, it should be noted, is an elaborate piece composed of finials and fretwork.

Music in Jogjakarta is played by the gamelan, an orchestra numbering usually about one or two dozen musicians, whose instruments are an assortment of elaborately carved and decorated xylophones, gongs, drums, and a violin-like instrument called the rebab. The voices of these instruments display reasonably great range both in terms of resources in scale (the xylophones) and in terms of the range of their values from the voice of the deepest gong to that of the highest note of the xylophone. Range is characteristically exploited fully in the synchronic musical structures, so that one is acutely aware of considerable tonal dispersion—in contrast to the closeness of the tonal spectrum in Guinea Coast music. This synchronic range of voice and of tonal dispersion is the similetic equivalent of maximal extension in space, and thus can be called extensionality. This is the style of Jogjanese music, just indeed as it is of dance, sculpture,

[2] This is presented as an over-generalization, for obviously there is individual variation in public behavior. But it is the truth of caricature which is pertinent here, a special category of truth whose merits are often overlooked nowadays, a tendency which often defeats the purposes of meaningful generalizations.

and costume; music also reaches to the extremities, posturing itself in its synchronicity.

This feature lends to the diachronic development of the music the same characteristic as that of the dance; music, too, is episodic, or serial. Under the circumstances, there can be no flowing development. Thus, the musical time is not continuously exploited, as it is in the music of Guinea Coast Africa. One is as aware with the music as he is with the dance that it is the value of discontinuity that is being expressed, that discontinuity is the part of that expressive mode creating whatever affect is being incarnated into the performance.

Synchronic structures are cast crisply and sharply delineated into the air, as carefully posed as the arms and legs of the dancer, giving the impression of two-dimensionality because of the crisply defined "outline" nature of the tones constituting the structure. Two-dimensionality must be viewed as a stylistic reinforcement, since it is subordinate to extensionalism. This causes it to appear more dramatically, to be different from the more naturalistic extensionality of the European ballet, where frontal as well as lateral extension is to be found. Tonal dispersions in the synchronic structures of music are the similetic equivalents of the reaching extensions of the body and its costumic accouterments in space. This is of the style of the affecting presence in Jogjakarta, and it is extensional. The phasal, partistic diachronic development of the dance and of music, the emphasis upon the points of juncture in the limbs and at the neck, and emphasis upon the synchronic musical structures are also similetically equivalent and are also stylistic elements. The stylistic-structural principle of the affecting presence in Jogjakarta is that of extensive discontinuity.

The Cultural Metaphoric Base
Evidenced in Other Behavior

The cultural metaphoric base—or at least as much of it as we have observed here—orders more than simply the temporal and spatial forms of the affecting presence. To one degree or another, it touches—I suspect—all temporal and spatial acts and works including those of social behavior as well. Although we will not touch upon social behavior here, we will pursue some possible further evidences of the cultural metaphoric base at work.

Among the Guinea Coast Africans, architecture was never a major activity; they did not build large, technically complex structures of enduring materials. Nor, with few notable exceptions, was the West Coast African moved to monument his land with other works intended to last from generation to generation, with the exception of the monolithic sculpture at Ife (fig. 31), which is a model of intensive continuity. Further, there is a sufficiently favorable fertile-land-to-inhabitant ratio that the earth need not show man's agricultural effects. Accordingly, one does not have, in the Nigerian environment, a strong sense of epoch devolving upon epoch and generation upon generation. Thus, there is in the land no omnipresent sense of accretion, nor of decay, nor of coming out of decay, only a sense of infinite present. But the bush, and the ghosts, and the road constitute a

179

kind of monumentation—timeless, spiritual, familial, and humane.

Ghosts and the bush as aspects of monumentation must be conceived of as related one to the other. The bush itself is an expression of force. It is unruly and has not in any significant sense submitted to the domination of man. The bush is land on the make—not harnessed, not sated. It is ever gravid and has not wearied of having borne. The bush does not need man, though man and his ghosts need the bush. The bush as an expression of force does not mean simply the great vernal force that seeds and bears or the fact that the bush is associated with deities. I refer to a more generalized force, the force that derives from burying outcasts in it, the force that inhabits certain trees, making them of particular potency. I refer, indeed, to the bush as Amos Tutuola has re-created it for us, committing the affect of belief and tradition to the pages of his books.

It is this bush which is inconceivable without ghosts and which exists monumented with the imaginative and spiritual energies of man. There is here, therefore, not so much a sense of the past of man, of the accretion of his epochs, as there is of his contemporaneity, of his continuity. All generations are omnipresent and the bush is ever virginal, ripe, and strong. The bush is body as well—from the bodies of its trees comes wine and from their branches, food; from the breast of the earth itself come yams. And with these foods, both of which on frequent occasions are used sacramentally, an identity between sacred and profane is forged.

A further part of the monumentation of Nigeria is the mythic— a force that often shapes what the eye perceives and is at the heart of what one feels when alone in the bush, that insinuates itself into his heart when he would be determinedly rational, and that is part of the air he breathes on hot nights, and that thinks, upon hearing strange sounds or when the drums beat, as Wordsworth did in another land, that the mighty being was awake.

And the roads—there is a basic at-homeness of the Nigerian toward the road. In the first place, it penetrates the bush, gives it definition, provides its entrance and its escape. The road is journey, it appears in proverb, and children play upon it; it is narrow, funneling goods and people with great intensity, particularly the women traders, from one market to another. The road in Nigeria is arterial, circulating the lifeblood of the economy.

180

43. Figures, Makond*

The road does not exist peripherally in fingers; it is vertebral, alimentary, functioning from here to there and from there to here. The road is part of the being of the people. And yet, as someone has observed in connection with Wole Soyinka's play, *The Road,* there is a fear of it. The road is also mystery; people are killed upon it. And the mammy lorries have painted upon their sides and backs sayings of despair or of faint hope, such as "God shall know his own."

The people are the being of the road—their hoarse laughter and shrill taunts or messages sometimes making great stretches of the road viable with their doings—boys, girls, men, women, bodies nearly nude, bodies swathed in enfolding robes, heads adorned, heads carrying enormous loads. The bodies of the Yoruba are full, visceral—and one sees them striding purposefully, the women always laden with parcels on their heads, children at their sides, babies on and in their bodies. Or one sees the Yoruba man or woman standing talking, arms akimbo, feet planted wide apart, the belly unrestrained, the laughter buoyant, the crisis intense, the contact full, corporeal. The road and the bush—indications of continuity; the economy of the road, the enfolding garments, the clutched and huddled babies—evidences of intension.

In Java it is very different. At the beginning, as with the Nigeria of the Yoruba, what stands out is the physical world in which the people live, for they have made of that an expression of themselves. What is most remarkable in Jogjakarta, in contrast with Ibadan, for example, is the density of monumentation. Those splendid, darkened ruins give one a strong sense of the accretion of man's experience in the world's time; they are remnants of the past, basically without function now, and they attest to history, to lapses, to empires faded, to the generationality of man.

Man has been infinitely operative upon the earth in Java, and his labors show. Not only are there the lichened temples and the crumbled palaces, but there are also the millennia of rice terraces that make one feel as though he had suddenly, miraculously, come to exist within the rigorous scalings of a contour map, or in the intricate and sharply etched ridges of a thumbprint which one ponders only to identify as that of time itself, pressed firmly and anciently upon the land.

Java is trod over, each grain, by the foot of man—from the great splayed pugs of *Homo soloensis* to the tiny brown pads of a present-day market woman. Java is inconceivable without the vast, succeeding waves of the past of man. If time is phasal in Java, it is distal as well; it is the reaching of all living men into the past and of all those past generations into the present. The points of juncture are manifest—the temples, the palaces, the ancient stone couches upon which royal loves were consummated and which are still forbidden to common men, and the rice contours, intricate in time as well as in space, exfoliating yet involuting upon themselves. And the eruptions of the volcano Merapi give in heart-like beats the long intervals of earth's own time—for earth, continuous; for man, discontinuous because of the phasality of his history, his awareness of the discreteness of past cultures.

One wishes to speak of many monuments, but mostly of Borobudur, a great sculpture built about A.D. 800 to the Buddha, soaring into the air. Composed of four galleries and three terraces, it depicts the estate of man, from the lowest to the highest, in reliefs on the galleries. The estate of man is also symbolized on the terraces by thirty-four, twenty-four, and sixteen stupas, culminating in the great central stupa of pure form which signifies the godhood of the Buddha and the aspirations of man. These stupas are the fingertips of the mind reaching for the eternal. And the topmost stupa is the finial of conceivable and of inconceivable reality, soaring pure and contentless into the sky, the consummation of all the squares, corners, forms, progressions, estates from which it arises but to which it is both the structural and the durational solution.

The total style of the people of Jogjakarta—clothed in their tight-fitting blouses and skirts, walking in their carefully tiny steps, keeping people at arm's length—is extensional; and because they exist of themselves and in the present, without the allegiance to the ancestors that characterized the Yoruba, the sense of discontinuity is keen about them.

Each Javanese household has one room at the entrance of the house which is, as far as I can tell, invariably furnished with a round table, served by four graceless and uncomfortable chairs, and a batik or two upon the wall. This is as far as one penetrates into the Javanese house; this is a completely public room. It shows nothing of the owner; it bears no stamp of his personality; it does not betray the family life that happens beyond this little room. The Yoruba compound, though enclosed by a wall, is

183

open and hospitable. The Yoruba compound embraces one; the Javanese reception room relegates one to the periphery.

There is something too about the preferred styles of fighting which reflects the Javanese distality (which is the extreme extensionality) and the Yoruba intensionality. The Javanese technique of interpersonal combat, called *puntsa'*, is the reinterpretation of the dance into offense. Naturally, given the offense-defense functions of personal combat, extensionality is transferred from a lateral plane to a frontal one. The presentational position is as follows: the fighter lifts and bends one leg at the knee, toes pointed down, and raises his arms, hands extended, parallel to the face so that the sharp edge of the palm faces the opponent. From that moment on, once the fight has commenced, it is a series of similarly extensive positions. The Yoruba on the other hand have as their preferred method of interpersonal combat wrestling, the intensivity of which hardly requires further comment.

The diets and method of food presentation of the two peoples similarly are in contrast, with the Javanese dinner consisting of a very great number of separate dishes, and the taste range extending from sweet through sour, from cool through hot. The Yoruba, on the other hand, tend to avoid great numbers of different dishes, and there is by no means as great an exploitation of the taste spectrum.

In sum, in the process of day-by-day *being* In strange lands, one *feels* the force of their affective and affecting way of life. As surely as a people express uniquely the content of their minds through a language and a logic, just as surely do they express in appropriate ways the content of their feelings. Through the affecting presence, through even what one might otherwise suspect is behavior wholly unrelated to affect, the content of the wellsprings of a people's sensibilities is disclosed, ever awake like a being giving to the people consciousness, identity, history. Thus, the cultural metaphoric base performs its role in humanizing man.

184

A Note on the Affecting Presence and Relativism

The view presented here envelops the affecting presence in all forms. That is, works of a given affect in one form in a certain culture are metaphorically of affecting equivalence to all other works of a similar affect in all other forms in the same culture. I have asserted that no such work can be wrenched from its cultural context without also in significant measure being divorced from its proper import, though it may subsequently be re-interpreted or affectingly re-invested in its host culture. It should be obvious that a view so committed to context is clearly relativistic. This view proceeds from the premise that culture is a whole, a system of systems (physical, rational, and affecting), that it is only with respect to that whole that the systems are related to one another, and that within any system the parts are also related with respect to that system. It is in terms of such relationships that significance is to be found and that understanding will come about.

The validity of such a view is self-evident, for no one will suggest that one can come to understand a person, object, or event in any way except in terms of causes and context. This relativism, then, is the view common sense would dictate to us; and although we are not guaranteed to come out all right if we adhere to it, at least we stand a chance of coming nearer to the truth through it—whereas we do not through any alternative procedures. But the question of relativism is a complex one, and although we cannot hope to identify or solve all the problems here, we can at least consider the major questions that are raised.

First to consider are the views I have developed of the affecting presence among the Yoruba and the Jogjanese. We do not know whether members of either group perceive their affecting works explicitly in such terms; we do know that they have not articulated such views. But let us assume that the principle of intensive continuity is not even suspected by the Yoruba and that the principle of extensive discontinuity has not been ascertained by the Jogjanese. These facts, although most interesting in themselves and of very great significance from a different point of view, are irrelevant to what I have developed here. The situation resembles that of a linguist who has done a phonemic analysis of Yoruba. The Yoruba may not be aware of the existence of the phonemes of their language—in fact they may even deny their existence once informed of them—but this does not invalidate the linguist's conclusions. The Yoruba may have a wholly different view of the phonological structure of their language, which may order the thinking about the language and adequately account for the data. But even this does not contradict the value or the validity of the linguist's work. Simply, there are two ways of ordering data or experience: one is in terms of the individual who is native to that culture, and the other is in terms of the individual who is a stranger to that culture. If a scholar is concerned to present data and systems in terms of the view from the inside, his approach is characterized as *cultural relativism*. If he presents data and systems from the latter point of view, his approach is *methodological relativism*. That the two approaches are sometimes confused, with the anthropologist maintaining that both are really the same and that both constitute cultural relativism, is no really respectable argument in favor of accepting the confusion.

In terms of cultural relativism, then, the conclusions here could not have been reached, for I do not know, for example, whether the principle of extensive discontinuity is recognized by the people of Jogjakarta. Because the principles I have isolated and described could not have been generated in terms of cultural relativism, an argument based in cultural relativism cannot reasonably be accepted as valid in objection to the identification and description of the principles.

187

The ethnographic and the xenographic perceptions of order among the diverse, affecting works of a culture reveal different kinds of information. The ethnographic perception is seldom if indeed ever of that system of affecting orders of metaphors and similetic equivalences. This comes about through the application of xenographic analysis. There are no differences concerning the validity of the two approaches; differences exist only with respect to the kind of knowledge generated.

In general, the pursuit of the ethnographic view will yield a wide spectrum of information, ranging from that which is *about* the affecting presence but irrelevant to its essential nature, to that which may be directly addressed to the essential nature of the affecting presence. Of whatever sort, however, information obtained by ethnographic procedures is by its very nature culturebound. Before it may be useful in perceiving the data in their own systems or contributing toward an understanding of human phenomena in general, ethnographic information must be arranged in a xenographic order, that is, in terms of a structure superordinate to the cultural knowledge of it.

I am not concerned here with the non-affecting aspects of the affecting presence which ethnographic analysis may reveal. Studies of the social role and function of the "artist," for example, bear no relevant relationship to the affecting presence in its own distinctive terms and are thus of no conceivable interest to us here. The study of systems of indigenous classification is one step nearer commanding our interest, for such systems concern the affecting presence, even though such systems typically are not constructed upon the basis of affecting considerations. Rather, they are more likely to be cast in terms of certain physical characteristics, uses, or subjects, such as *abstract and realistic, sacred and profane, representational and non-representational*. It is clear, however, that such information does not tell us much about the affecting presence; indeed, it tells us more about other aspects of the culture, such as the process of classification itself, or epistemology, or the relationship between the principles of classification and other factors in the culture.

The xenographic approach to the study of the affecting presence in a given culture, on the other hand, yields knowledge of the distinctive nature of the affecting presence—the cultural metaphoric base, the structure of the aesthemes of that culture. Such results produce knowledge, irrespective of any considerations of

188

fit between such knowledge and any internal system of classification, analysis of structure, or theories, if any, about the nature
and characteristics of the affecting presence or "work of art."
But both ethnographic and xenographic analyses may be used,
for relevant data of ethnographic analysis may be useful in the
identification of aesthemes—just as minimal ethnographic evidence is essential if one is to define the phonemes of a language.
The important point, however, is that xenographic analysis is
not unrelated to the data. It discloses inherent order, however
unknown to the indigenous peoples. Because this is true, field
work will, in the long run, clarify and validate (or reject) the
original hypotheses and will provide rich detail to illuminate the
affecting life of the culture. However, it is only the xenographic
approach which can be used if the data from diverse cultures are
to be brought together and studied toward the end of deriving
reliable, cross-cultural knowledge about the nature of the
affecting presence in human culture.

One must be especially aware, when considering the question
of relativism, to define the kind of relativism he means. There are
many reasons for this, some of which we have seen. Finally,
specification and analysis of terms are especially necessary in
defense against those few incautious souls to be encountered
here and there among the anthropologists who will reduce the
validity of knowledge to the context of a given culture, thus
delivering their discipline to the enigmas of solipsism, making
the practice of science impossible.

Conclusion

If anthropology is the study of human *being* (the profound implications of this word should not be missed) rather than merely of human behavior, which is but the cap of the iceberg of being—or perhaps better still, the radar reading of that cap—then the importance of what I have done in this study is greater than one might initially suspect. If the anthropologist is concerned not with human *being* but only with extrapolations and models, then these observations will have little meaning for him. Their importance must stand or fall in the context of some more humane discipline, one more concerned with the nature, the import, the relevance of being human, one which sees cultural variables as existential variables and cultural universals as fictive extrapolations from universals of being.

In any event, the anthropologist can no longer regard "the arts" as merely decorative, or the decorative as being of negligible or only ancillary importance. Rather he must see both as being in their own right, as existing in the universe of affect and thus as of the greatest importance in studying human *being* in culture. He must further study to perceive the sure yet subtle structure and dynamics of that universe. The implications for anthropology of what I have said here seem to me considerable. I have already pointed out how the organization of the universe of affect gives depth to the understanding of the nature of culture and how the approach here requires attention to the affecting

191

work as human action significant in its own terms rather than in other, irrelevant terms such as come about through the sociological, symbolic, psychiatric, technical, and other such accidental fallacies or reductions. I have further asserted that it is necessary, if we are to understand human *being* and the experience which is the base and touchstone to being, that we cease the tyranny of partism and recognize that human existence is not dominated solely by thoughtful and physical acts. If the anthropologist is to understand culture, then, he must take into account *all* of culture and not just part of it. In this regard, I do not know of any cultural anthropologists, but only of social anthropologists, psychological anthropologists, archaeologists, linguists.

To complete this list, we need the humanistic anthropologist and the philosophical anthropologist.[1] We need not be intimidated by charges of having violated "objectivity," or of lacking "hard" evidence, or of being victims of ethnocentrism. All evidence from exotic cultures is derived from paradigms of research that are culturebound in any case. *More* or *less* of ethnocentrism, subjectivity, or "softness" of fact is therefore the point, and excess is no more likely to characterize one area of anthropological practice than another. In any case, I fully suspect that what we have done here is no more ethnocentric than is phonemic analysis.

The significance of the affecting presence to the study of man is in terms of humanistic rather than of a sociological anthropology. The world of feeling, imagination, and intuition is the subject of our study, and from it our techniques derive. The objective of such an anthropology is an answer to the ancient question, *what is man?* This I view as far more interesting as well as more important than the question, *how does man behave?*

The implications of a humanistic anthropology for the understanding of man are very great indeed. It establishes a cross-cultural basis to the meaning and value of being. If the aim of the study of man is the understanding of man, a humanistic anthropology must inevitably make significant contributions to such a pursuit. Humanistic anthropology must proceed side by side with social anthropology, casting the abstract images of

[1] Alexander Pfänder, *Phenomenology of Willing and Motivation,* trans. Herbert Spiegelberg (Evanston: Northwestern University Press, 1967), pp. 75–85.

46. *Fragment, Nok.*

the social anthropologist upon the three-dimensional field of acting, feeling, and meaning. The anthropologist must no longer watch the shadows of reality cast upon the wall by the light from his own torch, not at least without realizing that his torch is not the light from the sun of understanding. Techniques of projection have improved since the day of Plato. Our images can become more reliable.

As we have known for centuries, non-corporeal man is composed of two equally real and very different parts—the mind and the spirit, which I choose to refer to as the "sensibilities" under the notion that it might arouse less antipathy in this secular age than the older term, which is actually much more meaningful particularly in relation to the affecting presence in Guinea Coast Africa. Both of these kinds of human activity, mental and spiritual, touch simultaneously upon many of our daily enterprises and upon our institutions. At the same time, there are certain kinds of experience and expression which are unique to one or the other of these two areas—algebra, with respect to the mind, and music, as an instance of the experience and expression of the spirit. Humanistic anthropology would devote its attention most ardently to the affairs of the spirit, and in so doing would breathe the breath of life and understanding into the forms identified and abstracted by the other kinds of anthropologists, or by other social scientists.

Although I have cast this study in terms of the affecting presence, and shall indeed permit it to stand in this way because of the special role enjoyed by the affecting presence, there is a vaster field of affective activity. It is in this total universe that the decorative design is a part of the affecting sensibility, as surely, though less powerfully, as a paramount affecting presence. In this universe, the affecting presence is thus but one kind of phenomenon among many. In this universe, the factors of importance are the cultural metaphoric base and its immediate function, the space-time metaphor, or the trope. These cause presentations in all reaches of affective action—from the Ilesha figure (fig. 3) through the wrestling style of the Yoruba.

In this universe of feeling, the affecting presence is a special thing, for whereas all objects and events in the realm of the sensibilities *are* by virtue of metaphor *what they convey*, the affecting presence is more than simply this. It is always, in one respect at least, the recipient of special treatment; unlike the decorative

194

element which enhances a surface or unlike a dress style, the affecting presence is a special kind of entity, an end in itself. It is a self-contained, self-sufficient, whole act of being in the affective universe and is to be distinguished from the symbol—as, for example, the Christian cross—that may have affecting dimensions. The affecting presence, then, is a very particular cultural reality, an entity, like the creator from whom it sprang and whom it perpetuates.

The affecting presence transcends both epoch and provenience, and it does so under the condition of being a presence. One need only look to the great public and private collections of ancient and modern, domestic and exotic art in Europe and America, for example, to assure himself of the validity of this observable property of the affecting presence. But if this were true only in these few places, the validity of the generalization might well be challenged. But in Sierra Leone, the Nomoli figure, carved by an earlier people, is given an important role in the agricultural life of the people. Terra cotta heads from ancient Ife still figure importantly in sacred rites.[2] Bamileke masks (fig. 32) have been found traded far along the Ogowe River in Gabon,[3] and the chi-wara (fig. 38) of the Bambara in Mali was chosen as a logo for the Nigerian journal, *Black Orpheus*.

The appropriate apperception of affecting works is, of course, characteristic only of those perceptors who are co-cultural with the work. I observed earlier that anyone can adequately perceive joy, compassion, pity, sorrow, etc., while admitting that the exact areas of definition given these areas of feeling might be differently mapped in different areas of the world. Everybody knows that some people behave differently from others in moments of embarrassment, which can cause the outsider to misinterpret such behavior. If the Japanese smiles when he is embarrassed, we must reinterpret our notion of the smile, when speaking of Japanese culture, and add a new dimension to the manifestation of embarrassment if we are to understand either in a way that is anywhere near adequate. Further, the Bacham mask is said to inspire terror in those who are co-cultural with it, whereas for others it does nothing of the sort, causing,

[2] Frank Willett, *Ife and the History of West African Sculpture* (New York: McGraw-Hill Book Co., 1967), plates 69, 70.

[3] Letter written by Adam Pollock in "A Propos," *African Arts* 3 (1968): 94–95.

instead, great admiration for the formal inventiveness and beauty —a special category of the appeal of the affecting work—that characterize it.

Even were it not for the fact that the provinces of the emotions are differently defined among different peoples or that what excites one emotion one place may not excite the same emotion elsewhere, it remains that though we may appreciate the dignity and beauty of the Anyi mother (fig. 33), for example, we do not do so in terms of the same aesthetics of intensive continuity. The affecting presence can be divorced from its native time and place, but when this is done it is thus subject to perception only by means of an affective reinterpretation which may or may not approximate the appropriate apperception of it. If it does, it does so purely by the most accidental of circumstances.

The complete, total affecting presence is a web of tensions— tension between form and formlessness, intension and extension, continuity and discontinuity, physical conformation (spatial or temporal) and emotion, media and metaphor, and the ordinary and the extraordinary. Further, it is a complex of metaphoric levels, all coming simultaneously to focus in the work—the universal metaphor, the cultural metaphoric base, the space/time metaphor, the objective metaphor, the formal metaphor, and the objective correlative. It is a wonder, but no surprise, that the affecting work may be described as a presence, an entity, which though it is native to a time and place, is not the prisoner of either. At the same time, however, the affecting presence is as subject to misunderstanding—or, indeed, understanding—out of its own culture as its creator himself might be.

The world of the affecting presence is as subject to stability and change as the mental and material cultural worlds are. Frank Willett points out that some of the characteristics we observe in recent Yoruba carving were already present in the carving of Nok culture two thousand years ago.[4] We have already seen something of the continuity of affecting content and attitudes in the affecting works of the Javanese of Jogjakarta. In speaking of *Weltgefühl*, Claire Holt, stating that "works of art convey a special emotive mood which is undoubtedly closely linked with the moral order—of a phase of history and of a cultural area," goes on to note: "Through the ages changing moral orders

[4] Willett, *Ife and West African Sculpture*, p. 182.

196

have evoked . . . [numerous, successive] attitudes of Indonesia's people. . . . None of these attitudes and its resultant patterns of behavior have ever necessarily excluded any or all of the others. Today in both urban and rural Indonesia one is sure to find a mixture of all those attitudes in various combinations and proportions."[5] In Western Europe and the United States, on the other hand, the same degree of aesthetic conservatism is not to be noted. Quite the contrary is the case, as is known by those with even the most casual acquaintance with the history of European civilizations.

Bearing in mind the experiences of the European and American civilizations, one can make some general statements about the affecting presence among the Yoruba and the Jogjanese. The principles of intensive continuity and extensive discontinuity might indeed be regarded as cultural foci, if one wishes to classify them according to traditional anthropological notions of the nature of culture, since they are unconscious and since they order the world of affective and affecting activity, the spirit of the people. However, there is no evidence that they are especially amenable to experimentation under normal conditions, a circumstance which is cited as characterizing the area of culture focus, for wild experimentation has characterized the expressions of the affecting presence in Europe and America but not in Jogjakarta or among the Yoruba—not, at least, in the period of the recent traditional with which we have here been concerned, though there is considerable evidence of experimentation now among painters, sculptors, and writers. Further, it is said of the cultural focus that in times of culture contact, it is notably resistant to change. The evidence on this point seems clear. Both the Yoruba and the Javanese of Jogjakarta have been under intense contact as colonies of European powers for several centuries, and the affecting forms suffered little change. Indeed, the evidence could be read to support this aspect of focus, such as the slaves taking with them to the New World their native systems of feeling, and accordingly producing West African affecting forms in the New World. On the other hand, however, the case is different in situations of non-colonial acculturation, and contemporary experimentation shows that

[5] Claire Holt, *Art in Indonesia: Continuities and Change* (Ithaca: Cornell University Press, 1967), pp. 5–6.

neither the principle of intensive continuity nor that of extensive discontinuity shows great determination to endure in the face of present-day Westernization of the affecting forms brought about through the educational system. There are, of course, many factors which must be taken into account in considering this more permissive situation, notably, of course, the absence of inimical foreign powers occupying one's land and threatening one's culture. Then, too, there are the staggering differences in the technology of communications which would serve to dress up and to speed up the acculturative process.

In general, it would appear that in a culture with great inner integrity, one which is not in the throes of change brought about by intensive contact, there is a prevalent cultural metaphoric base and a narrow range of stylistic and structural diversity. In situations of intense inter-cultural contact, marked also by an absence of duress, stylistic range will be increased and, due to the influence of imported affecting presences, even the cultural metaphoric base may suffer significant change. This, indeed, was the case when West African works were imported into Europe and incorporated into early twentieth-century painting and sculpture. Though there was some reinterpretation of these affecting forms, so that the abstractions and geometricizations would be more consonant with our European preferences, there was nonetheless some effect upon a certain segment of the cultural metaphoric base such that through the period of the twenties and thirties in sculpture and in decor and under the name of "modernistic," abstractions and planes were everywhere to be encountered. And the influences upon our music and our dance are obvious.

It is possible, as a further point, for a culture to become so concerned with the physical form of the affecting presence that its feelingful import is lost sight of. Under these circumstances, the work, in essence divested of its affecting charge, becomes of interest in purely aesthetic terms; and as a result, decadence sets in. Physical form becomes elaborated beyond all point of affecting purposes, and the rococo develops. In such a period, the affecting presence is ameliorated and its voice, where it exists at all, is shrill and nears the vacuous. In an age of belief in the affecting presence, however, the decadent, the emptily mannered, the rococo never come into being. In these periods, the affecting presence will eloquently proclaim its identity,

199

whether in formal homogeneity or heterogeneity, and it will be heard through all lands and all times.

The human sensibilities are as subject as social behavior to those generalizations about uniformities and those characteristics of form and process which we call culture. I have made such generalizations here. There is yet another to be made, however. It is clear that these patterns we have observed are not conscious. The Yoruba do not know of the existence of intensive continuity, nor in all probability do they perceive the similetic identities among their forms, any more than they know of the phonemes in their language. Nor do the Javanese of Jogjakarta know about the principle of extensive discontinuity, though they will accept affecting works or behavior expressing it and reject those denying it. It is quite likely that, aside from various common interests in substance, the practitioners of the various forms during the Romantic period of European culture did not know of the principles and patterns which similarly gave a common structure and style to their music, dance, architecture, literature, painting, and sculpture, and similetically equated them.

That such patterns are not conscious is hardly surprising to the anthropologist, who perceives and articulates the presence in a culture of many patterns of which those native to that culture are not aware, or if so, only dimly. He has been content to say that such patterns are carried "below the level of consciousness," and he has had to rest there—not, perhaps, quite content. But what does it mean when one asserts that a pattern is carried below the level of consciousness? *How* is it carried? What *carries* it? If it exists and is unconscious, what caused it to exist and why is it unconscious? Did someone at some time invent the pattern? And did it subsequently become unconscious (it being taken for granted that the pattern could hardly have been "invented" unconsciously)? We know that behavior in society cannot be totally random if culture is to exist, but why do such master patterns exist, master patterns which order into identical structures activities which are as vastly different as sculpture and music? Surely no one worked out the equivalences of the similetic metaphor and proceeded to example it in each form.

When we consider such questions, we perceive first that we

200

48. *Seated figure, Tada, Yoruba.*

have in some respects been put on a false track. To say that the social structure *qua* structure may be carried "below" the level of consciousness means only that although all the data exist in consciousness, they have never been brought together into a whole picture. The same is true of the grammar of a language which, even though the language is unwritten and though there are grammarians, asserts itself and channels new linguistic phenomena into harmonious lines and prevents the making of "mistakes." The evidence for the grammar is there, but it has not been extrapolated and formulated into a system of statements concerning what is and what is not done in the language. Such principles are not carried *below* the level of consciousness; they are simply not carried *in* the consciousness. This is fairly simple: one distinct category of behavior, which by definition may not be random if the intentions toward which the behavior is directed are to be fulfilled, has its order perceived.

The case is different, however, in the instance of affecting actions where several distinct categories of form, each exhibiting its own patterned regularities, can be demonstrated to be acting out a common affective injunction. The system is to be perceived from the data, and it may thus be argued that the case is not different, that only the scale or the complexity is changed and not the nature of the basic, cultural phenomenon. This is all right in a sense, since the argument presupposes that affect is a category and that the various arts are, in effect, subcategories. But although it is one thing to structure to a common pattern all one's speaking, it is quite another to structure to a common pattern all one's affecting activities in surface, volume, color, tone, movement, word, relationality, and experience. That a master pattern, or complex of patterns, so orders such diverse data staggers the mind, and that the complex has never been totally displayed as a system of abstract principles, nor perhaps even accurately guessed at as we have tried to do here, is testimony to its subtlety. The system is not to be perceived in the data of one medium but in all the media of affecting expression, or more precisely in their relationships and identities. Much generalization is required here. This kind of understanding comes through recognizing a master plan at work. The master plan exists in that faculty of man which feels and which enacts his feelings. The evidence for this resides in the records of the great historical shifts in systems of perception and feeling, as

202

from Classicism to Romanticism. Here, without the explicit formulations of a system detailing how each of the arts must subscribe to the tenets of the new belief, each art did nonetheless harmoniously work itself out so that taken as a whole they reflected—we must assume as a total, organic system exhibiting similetic identities throughout—indeed constituted the spirit of the age, the new feeling. There thus appears to be, in this case at least, a "mental" culture which is not wholly resident in behavioral fact but transcends it.

It is at this point that it becomes relevant to look to the work done by Sir John Eccles [6] and others in neurophysiology. Working with subjects in whom either surgically or experimentally there was a separation between the two hemispheres of the brain, it was discovered that the dominant hemisphere of the brain, the left in a right-handed person, appears to relate solely to consciousness and in particular to be the center of language (symbolism), which is a chief mediator of consciousness. The recessive half, on the other hand, is concerned with formal and spatial problems. Thus such a subject (right-handed) can solve formal problems with his left hand that he cannot solve with his right and can write words and numbers with his right hand, a feat he cannot achieve with his left. One wonders whether the cultural metaphoric base which orders time and space to a common model is not to be found here, in the recessive hemisphere of the brain, and whether, as the affecting presence is not symbolic, it is not the time/space expression in direct terms of that hemisphere. In this case, it would appear not so much that the recessive hemisphere is unconscious—consciousness being defined in terms of symbolism and particularly, in Eccles' book, in terms of language—as that it is a-conscious. This is an area of research of great importance to the future study of the affecting presence and to the study of culture as well—both of which may indeed have relevance to that brain research itself, if only to pose trenchant and interesting questions.

Meanwhile, we must know that man, since his inception, has been expressing himself and protecting those expressions. And, all told, up until this present century, he has written perhaps nearly as often in the attempt to explain the great work of feeling as he has to explain the objects of nature. I hope I have managed

[6] Sir John Eccles, *The Brain and the Unity of Conscious Experience* (Cambridge: At the University Press, 1965).

203

to perceive something of the nature of the affecting work in general, and in particular to sketch in some of the contours of the affecting universe of two peoples. If I have done so, perhaps their lives and their cultures will appear a little more fully dimensioned.

Bibliography

Achebe, Chinua. "English and the African Writer." *Transition* 18 (1965).

Beier, Ulli. "Fagunwa: A Yoruba Novelist." *Black Orpheus* 17 (1965).

Eccles, Sir John. *The Brain and the Unity of Conscious Experience.* Cambridge: At the University Press, 1965.

Fagg, William B. *Tribes and Forms in African Art.* New York: Tudor Publishing Co., 1965.

Fagg, William B., and Plass, Margaret, *African Sculpture.* New York: E. P. Dutton & Co., Dutton Vista Pictureback, 1964.

Fagunwa, Daniel O. *The Forest of a Thousand Daemons: A Hunter's Saga,* trans. Wole Soyinka. London: Thomas Nelson & Sons, 1968.

Harper, Peggy. "Dance Studies." *African Notes,* vol. 4. Ibadan, Nigeria: Institute of African Studies, University of Ibadan, 1968, p. 22.

Herskovits, Melville J. *The Human Factor in a Changing Africa.* New York: Alfred A. Knopf, 1962.

Holt, Claire. *Art in Indonesia: Continuities and Change.* Ithaca: Cornell University Press, 1967.

Horton, Robin. *Kalabari Sculpture.* Apapa, Nigeria: Department of Antiquities, 1965.

Langer, Susanne K. *Philosophy in a New Key: A Study in the Symbolism of Reason, Rite, and Art,* 3rd ed. Cambridge, Mass.: Harvard University Press, 1957.

Lindfors, Bernth. "Characteristics of Yoruba and Igbo Prose Styles in English." Paper given at the Contemporary African Literatures seminar, held at the annual meeting of the Modern Language Association of America, New York, December 27, 1968.

Merleau-Ponty, Maurice. *Phenomenology of Perception.* New York: Humanities Press, Inc., 1962.

_____. *The Primacy of Perception and Other Essays.* Evanston: Northwestern University Press, 1964.

205

Merriam, Alan P. *The Anthropology of Music*. Evanston: Northwestern University Press, 1964.

Nwankwo, Nkem. *Danda*. London: Andre Deutsch, 1964.

O'Malley, Glenn. *Shelley and Synesthesia*. Evanston: Northwestern University Press, 1964.

Pfänder, Alexander. *Phenomenology of Willing and Motivation*, trans. Herbert Spiegelberg. Evanston: Northwestern University Press, 1967.

Thompson, Robert F. "Esthetics in Traditional Africa." *Art News* 66 (1968).

Tutuola, Amos. *The Palm-Wine Drinkard*. London: Faber and Faber Ltd., 1962.

Veatch, Henry B. *Two Logics: The Conflict between Classical and Neo-Analytic Philosophy*. Evanston: Northwestern University Press, 1969.

Wheelwright, Philip. *Burning Fountain: A Study in the Language of Symbolism*, rev. ed. Bloomington: Indiana University Press, 1968.

———. *Metaphor and Reality*. Bloomington: Indiana University Press, 1962.

Willett, Frank. *Ife and the History of West African Sculpture*. New York: McGraw-Hill Book Co., 1967.

Index

207

114–16; continuity in, 110, 122; discussion of, 16; distribution of media in, 15; experience as medium in, 126; intension(ality) in, 110–14; intensive continuity in, 108–14, 124–25; interest in verticality in, 106, 108; lack of portraiture in, 104; masks, 104; media characteristics in, 108–26; patterning in, 16; situation(ality) as medium in, 118; smooth finish prized in, 166; structural variability limited in, 16–17; surface in, xvii, 116–18, 166; volume in, 108–16; wood-carving tradition in, 103

A Note on the Author

Robert Plant Armstrong is professor and director of Northwestern University Press. He received his B.A. in English from the University of Arizona, his M.A. from the Writers Workshop at the State University of Iowa, and his Ph.D. in anthropology from Northwestern University in 1957. In his varied career he has won the Phoebe M. Bogan Poetry Prize at the University of Arizona in 1944, has been an English instructor at Balai Bahasa Inggeris in Jogjakarta, Indonesia, in 1955–56, has published several articles in anthologies on anthropology, and has lectured at the chief centers of African studies on theoretical anthropology. *The Affecting Presence* is his first book.

UNIVERSITY OF ILLINOIS PRESS